MathFlare

Name: ___________________________

Class: ____________

Teacher: ___________________________

Introduction

As parents and educators, we recognize the pivotal role mathematics plays in shaping a child's academic journey and future success. Yet, the path to mathematical proficiency can often seem daunting, fraught with challenges and complexities. That's where the transformative power of MathFlare Workbooks shine through, illuminating the way forward with clarity, precision, and purpose.

Introducing MathFlare Workbooks – a beacon of guidance, a testament to excellence, and a catalyst for achievement. Crafted with meticulous care and expertise, MathFlare Workbooks stand as paragons of educational excellence, designed to nurture young minds, ignite a passion for learning, and develop a deep-rooted understanding of mathematical concepts.

Picture this: your child eagerly delves into the pages of Mathflare Workbook, greeted by a step-by-step guide illuminated with vivid examples that demystify complex mathematical concepts. With each turn of the page, they embark on a journey of discovery, encountering thoughtfully curated practice questions that reinforce learning and hone problem-solving skills. And when they unveil the answers to those very questions, a sense of accomplishment blossoms within them – a tangible reward for their hard work and dedication.

But MathFlare Workbooks are more than just tools for learning; they are pathways to comprehension, fostering a deep-seated understanding of mathematical concepts through a sequential, logical flow. From fundamental principles to advanced problem-solving strategies, every chapter builds upon the last, ensuring a robust foundation upon which future knowledge can be constructed.

As parents, we yearn for nothing more than to see our children thrive, to witness the spark of inspiration ignited within them as they conquer academic challenges with confidence and poise. MathFlare Workbooks serve as partners in this noble endeavor, offering not just practice questions, but the keys to unlocking a world of opportunity.

And for teachers, MathFlare Workbooks stand as invaluable allies in the quest to cultivate mathematical proficiency in the classroom. With answers readily available, instructors can focus on guiding and nurturing their students, confident in the knowledge that MathFlare Workbooks provide a solid framework upon which to build.

In the pages of MathFlare Workbooks, we find not just the promise of academic excellence, but the seeds of a brighter tomorrow. So let us embrace the power of mathematics, let us champion the journey of learning, and let us pave the way for a generation of young minds poised to shape the world. With MathFlare Workbooks as our guide, the possibilities are infinite, and the future, bright.

Table of Contents

MathFlare
Grade 2
MATH WORKBOOK
Step by Step Guide and Essential Practice with Answers
Addition Subtraction
Multiplication
Place Value and Expanded Notations
Geometry
MathFlare Publishing

MathFlare
Grade 2-3
MATH WORKBOOK
Step by Step Guide and Essential Practice with Answers
Addition Subtraction
Multiplication and Division
Place Value and Expanded Notations
Geometry
MathFlare Publishing

MathFlare
Grade 3
MATH WORKBOOK
Step by Step Guide and Essential Practice with Answers
Multiplication and Division
Decimals
Place Value and Expanded Notations
Fractions and Geometry
MathFlare Publishing

MathFlare
Grade 1
MATH WORKBOOK
Step by Step Guide and Essential Practice with Answers
Counting and Numbers
Addition and Subtraction
Place Value and Expanded Notations
Understanding Time
MathFlare Publishing

MathFlare
Grade 1-2
MATH WORKBOOK
Step by Step Guide and Essential Practice with Answers
Counting and Numbers
Addition and Subtraction
Place Value and Expanded Notations
Understanding Time
MathFlare Publishing

MathFlare
Grade 3-4
MATH WORKBOOK
Step by Step Guide and Essential Practice with Answers
Addition Subtraction
Multiplication Division
Place Value and Expanded Notations
Fractions and Geometry
MathFlare Publishing

MathFlare
Grade 4
MATH WORKBOOK
Step by Step Guide and Essential Practice with Answers
Addition Subtraction
Multiplication Division
Place Value and Expanded Notations
Fractions and Geometry
MathFlare Publishing

MathFlare
Grade 4-5
MATH WORKBOOK
Step by Step Guide and Essential Practice with Answers
Multiplication Division
Place Value and Expanded Notations
Fractions and Geometry
Unit Conversion
MathFlare Publishing

MathFlare
Grade 5
MATH WORKBOOK
Step by Step Guide and Essential Practice with Answers
Multiplication Division
Place Value and Expanded Notations
Fractions and Geometry
Unit Conversion
MathFlare Publishing

MathFlare
Grade 5-6
MATH WORKBOOK
Step by Step Guide and Essential Practice with Answers
Multiplication Division
Place Value and Expanded Notations
Fractions and Geometry
Units and Statistics
MathFlare Publishing

MathFlare
Grade 6
MATH WORKBOOK
Step by Step Guide and Essential Practice with Answers
Integers and Statistics
Arithmetic and Pre-Algebra
Fractions and Geometry
Ratio and Percentage
MathFlare Publishing

MathFlare
Grade 6-7
MATH WORKBOOK
Step by Step Guide and Essential Practice with Answers
Arithmetic and Pre-Algebra
Ratio, Percent Proportion
Geometry
Statistics
MathFlare Publishing

MathFlare
Grade 7
MATH WORKBOOK
Step by Step Guide and Essential Practice with Answers
Pre-Algebra
Ratio, Percent Proportion
Geometry
Statistics
MathFlare Publishing

MathFlare
Grade 7-8
MATH WORKBOOK
Step by Step Guide and Essential Practice with Answers
Pre-Algebra
Ratio, Percent Proportion
Geometry and Cartesian Plane
Statistics
MathFlare Publishing

MathFlare
Grade 8-9
MATH WORKBOOK
Step by Step Guide and Essential Practice with Answers
Pre-Algebra
Ratio, Proportion and Percentage
Linear Equations
Geometry and Cartesian Plane
MathFlare Publishing

MathFlare
Grade 8
MATH WORKBOOK
Step by Step Guide and Essential Practice with Answers
Pre-Algebra
Percentage
Linear Equations
Geometry
MathFlare Publishing

Multiplication and Division

Multiplication

Multiplication is an easy way of adding numbers together quickly. Instead of adding the same number repeatedly, we use multiplication to find the total much faster.

For instance, rather than adding 2 + 2 + 2 + 2 + 2, we can multiply 2 by 5 to get the same result: 2 x 5 = 10.

Here, the first number (2) is called the multiplicand, second number (5) is the multiplier. The answer we get, in this case, 10, is called the product.

Let's think of multiplication as repeated addition.

Take 2 x 5, for example. It means adding 2 together five times, which we can illustrate as: 2 + 2 + 2 + 2 + 2 = 10

Multiplication can also be visualized as groups of objects. Imagine we have 2 groups, each containing 5 oranges.

To find the total number of oranges, we multiply the number of groups (2) by the number of oranges in each group (5):

2 groups of 5 oranges = 10 oranges

Expressed as multiplication: 2 x 5 = 10

In summary, multiplication offers various ways to approach it: through repeated addition or by envisioning groups of objects. It's a powerful tool that makes solving math problems much quicker and more efficient!

We can also use the following table to quickly remember multiplication facts. The intersection of two points shows the product of two numbers.

For instance, the product of 5 x 6 = 30, or 6 x 5 = 30.

	1	2	3	4	5	6	7	8	9	10
1	1	2	3	4	5	6	7	8	9	10
2	2	4	6	8	10	12	14	16	18	20
3	3	6	9	12	15	18	21	24	27	30
4	4	8	12	16	20	24	28	32	36	40
5	5	10	15	20	25	30	35	40	45	50
6	6	12	18	24	30	36	42	48	54	60
7	7	14	21	28	35	42	49	56	63	70
8	8	16	24	32	40	48	56	64	72	80
9	9	18	27	36	45	54	63	72	81	90
10	10	20	30	40	50	60	70	80	90	100

<u>Multiplication: 3 x 3</u>

Let's solve problems from exercises:

$$\begin{array}{r} 422 \\ \times\ 777 \\ \hline +\quad 2954 \\ +\quad 2954 \\ +\ \underline{2954} \\ =\ 327894 \end{array}$$

<u>Multi Digit Multiplication</u>

$$\begin{array}{r} 38{,}518 \\ \times\qquad 295 \\ \hline +\quad 192590 \\ +346662 \\ +\underline{77036} \\ =1362810 \end{array}$$

<u>Long Division and Remainders</u>

Division is like the opposite of multiplication. It's all about sharing or distributing items equally among a certain number of groups or people.

When we divide one number by another, we're essentially splitting a number into equal parts. We're figuring out how many groups of a certain size can be made from that number.

For instance, let's divide 20 by 4.

When we divide 20 by 4, we're essentially asking, "How many groups of size 4 can we make from 20?"

Now, there are several parts or terms involved in the division process:

- **Dividend:** This is the number being divided, which in this case, is 20.

- **Divisor:** This is the number we're dividing by, which is 4.

- **Quotient:** This is the answer we get after dividing. It tells us how many groups of divisors can be made from the dividend. In this case, the answer is 5.

- **Remainder:** when the divisor doesn't evenly divide the dividend, we get the remainder.

So, when we divide 20 by 4, we found out that 5 groups of 4 can be made from 20.

Let's solve problems from exercises:

$$
\begin{array}{r}
4 \\
4\,)\overline{16} \\
-16 \\
\hline
0
\end{array}
\qquad
\begin{array}{r}
42 \\
12\,)\overline{504} \\
-48 \\
\hline
24 \\
-24 \\
\hline
0
\end{array}
\qquad
\begin{array}{r}
477 \\
6\,)\overline{2{,}862} \\
-24 \\
\hline
46 \\
-42 \\
\hline
42 \\
-42 \\
\hline
0
\end{array}
\qquad
\begin{array}{r}
8{,}965 \text{ R1} \\
9\,)\overline{80{,}686} \\
-72 \\
\hline
86 \\
-81 \\
\hline
58 \\
-54 \\
\hline
46 \\
-45 \\
\hline
1
\end{array}
$$

<u>Using the Power of 10</u>

Using the powers of 10, 100, and 1000 makes multiplying and dividing by these numbers very convenient. Let's illustrate with examples:

Multiplying by Powers of 10:

- To multiply a number by 10, simply move the decimal point one place to the right.

$$5 \times 10 = 50$$

- To multiply a number by 100, move the decimal point two places to the right.

$$5 \times 100 = 500$$

- To multiply a number by 1000, move the decimal point three places to the right.

$$5 \times 1000 = 5000.$$

Dividing by Powers of 10:

- To divide a number by 10, simply move the decimal point one place to the left.

$$50 \div 10 = 5$$

- To divide a number by 100, move the decimal point two places to the left.

$$500 \div 100 = 5$$

- To divide a number by 1000, move the decimal point three places to the left.

$$5000 \div 1000 = 5$$

Using the powers of 10, 100, and 1000 makes multiplying and dividing by these numbers simple and straightforward.

<u>Multiplication and Division Word Problems</u>

Anthony can run four laps in 1 hour. How many laps can Anthony run in 18 hours?

$$
\begin{array}{r}
4 \\
\times\, 18 \\
\hline
+\, 3\,2 \\
+\, 4 \\
\hline
=\, 7\,2
\end{array}
$$

1 hour 4 laps
how many laps can he run in 18 hours?

Anthony can run 72 laps in 18 hours

How many 12 cm pieces of rope can you cut from a rope that is 420 cm long?

```
      35
  12) 520
     -36
      60
     -60
       0
```

35 pieces can be cut

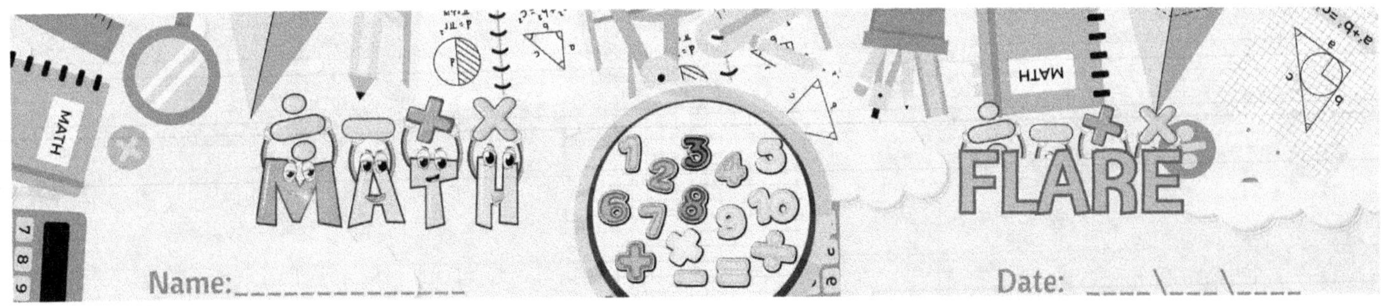

Multiplication (3 Digit)

Find the product.

1. 216 × 637	2. 682 × 392	3. 574 × 574	4. 748 × 267
5. 705 × 359	6. 953 × 312	7. 358 × 240	8. 954 × 433
9. 557 × 199	10. 176 × 682	11. 523 × 129	12. 930 × 429

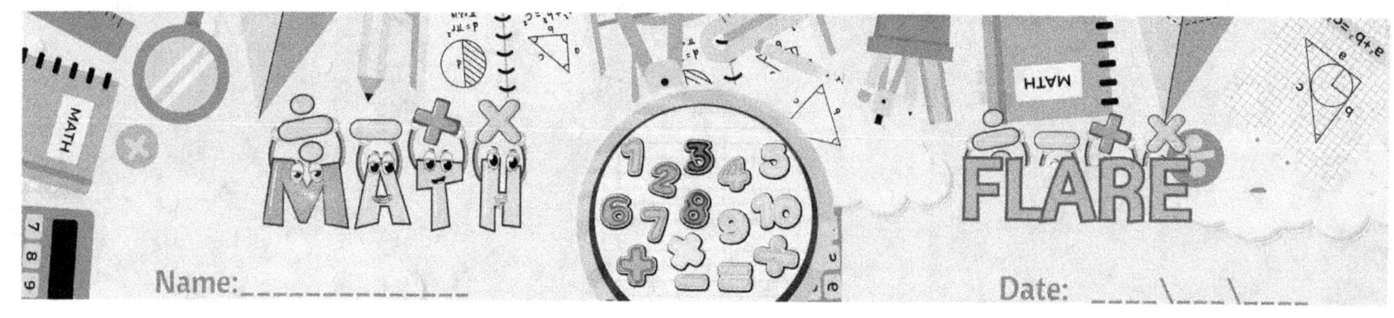

13. 273 × 521	14. 469 × 954	15. 623 × 343	16. 257 × 845
17. 235 × 677	18. 171 × 239	19. 963 × 787	20. 691 × 758
21. 111 × 985	22. 573 × 519	23. 216 × 754	24. 357 × 439

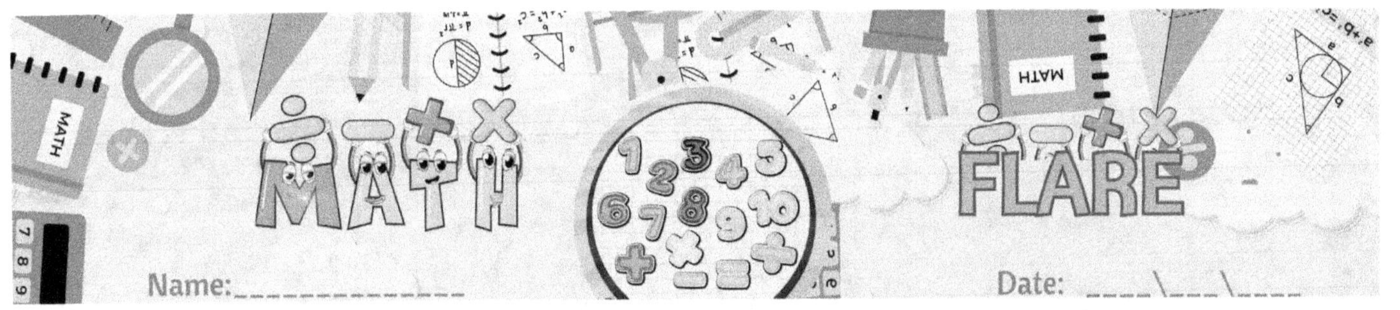

25. 561
   × 609

26. 969
   × 293

27. 163
   × 513

28. 859
   × 187

29. 705
   × 353

30. 219
   × 153

31. 205
   × 793

32. 643
   × 462

33. 202
   × 209

34. 177
   × 680

35. 169
   × 815

36. 469
   × 769

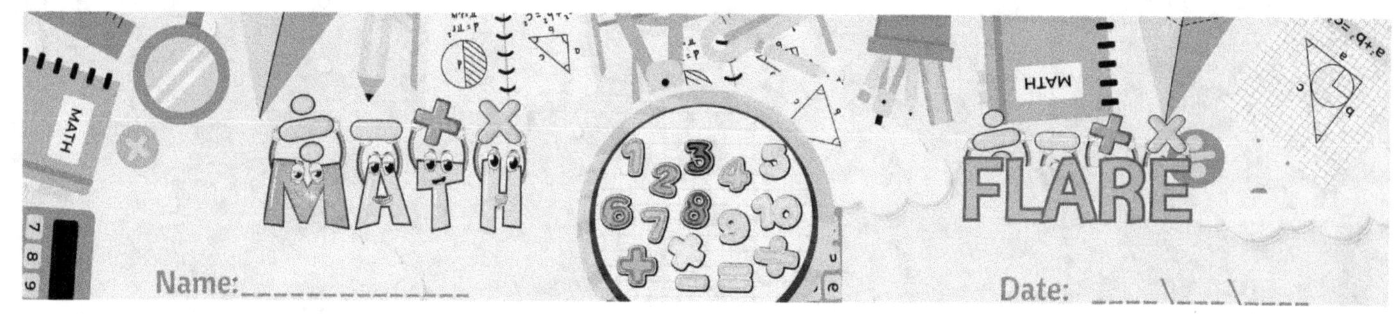

37. 508 × 416	38. 671 × 537	39. 555 × 511	40. 313 × 518
41. 264 × 130	42. 493 × 114	43. 373 × 963	44. 781 × 721
45. 816 × 983	46. 533 × 709	47. 668 × 638	48. 654 × 317

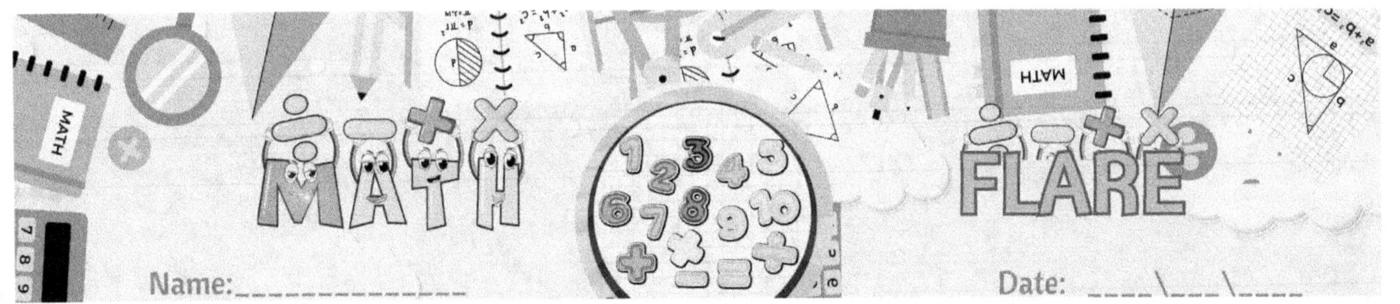

| 49. | 443
× 211 | 50. | 417
× 107 | 51. | 676
× 676 | 52. | 370
× 745 |

| 53. | 239
× 300 | 54. | 785
× 746 | 55. | 841
× 423 | 56. | 631
× 294 |

| 57. | 140
× 700 | 58. | 888
× 174 | 59. | 401
× 629 | 60. | 189
× 239 |

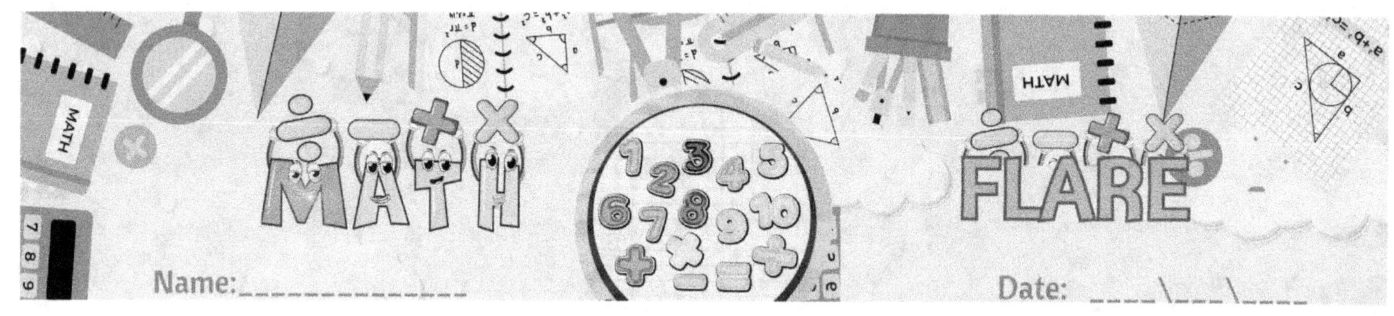

61. 426
× 455

62. 863
× 184

63. 383
× 759

64. 202
× 869

65. 762
× 454

66. 194
× 444

67. 194
× 306

68. 841
× 587

69. 759
× 746

70. 874
× 173

71. 278
× 135

72. 879
× 494

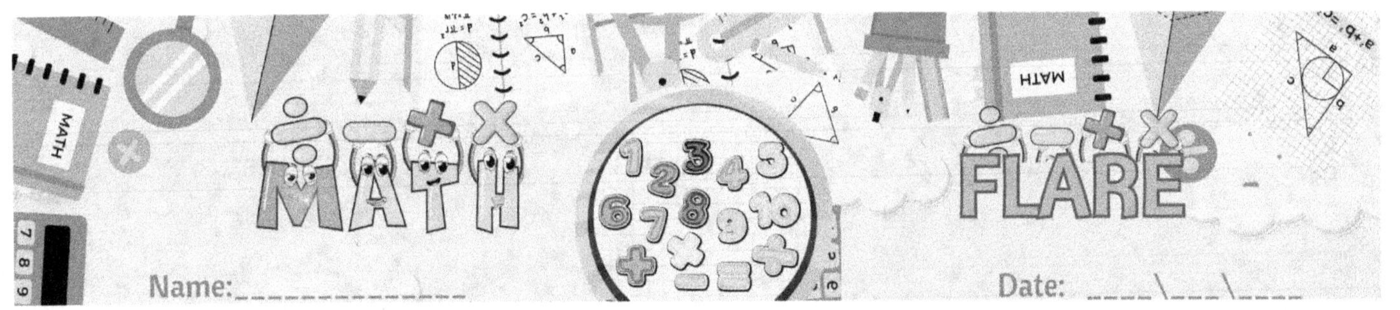

73. 452 × 338	74. 669 × 967	75. 749 × 579	76. 915 × 813
77. 122 × 278	78. 680 × 321	79. 812 × 286	80. 462 × 479
81. 198 × 915	82. 983 × 487	83. 329 × 287	84. 200 × 833

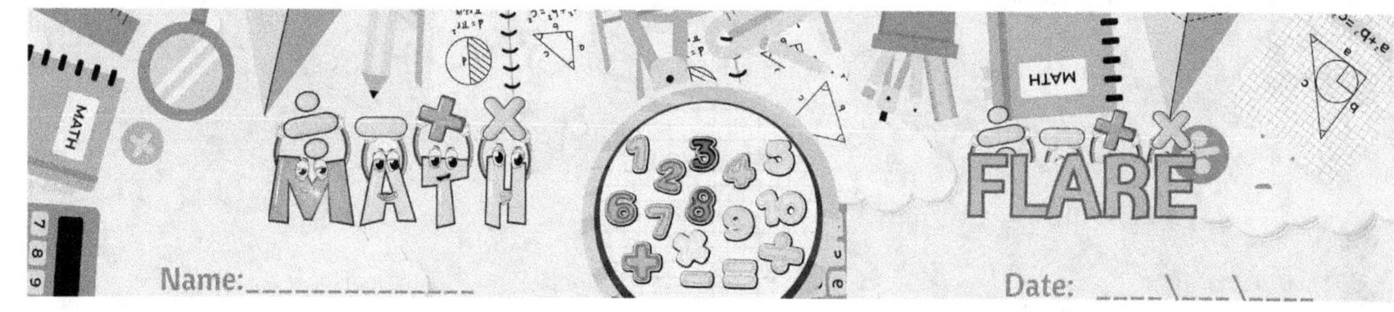

85. 858 × 401	86. 414 × 653	87. 754 × 116	88. 960 × 391
89. 575 × 469	90. 731 × 144	91. 190 × 234	92. 220 × 282
93. 538 × 380	94. 422 × 916	95. 625 × 620	96. 774 × 574

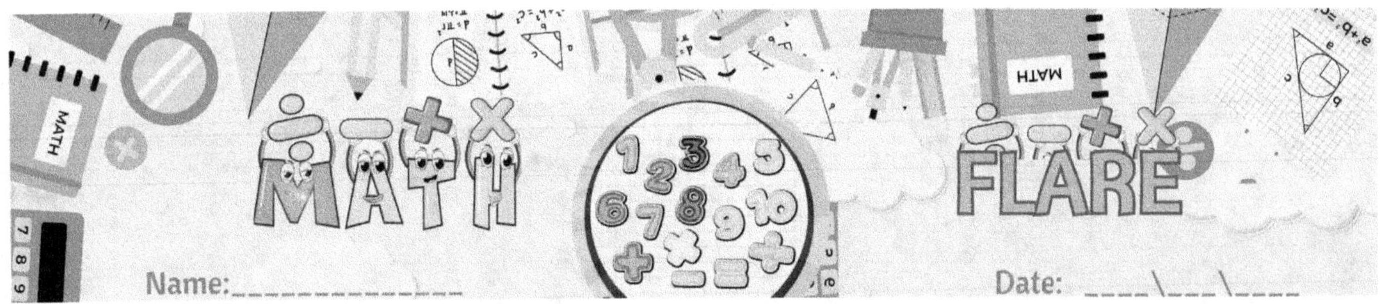

97. 384
   × 495

98. 974
   × 362

99. 151
   × 492

100. 265
   × 265

101. 239
    × 834

102. 208
    × 448

103. 265
    × 362

104. 159
    × 107

105. 317
    × 388

106. 745
    × 443

107. 554
    × 418

108. 389
    × 963

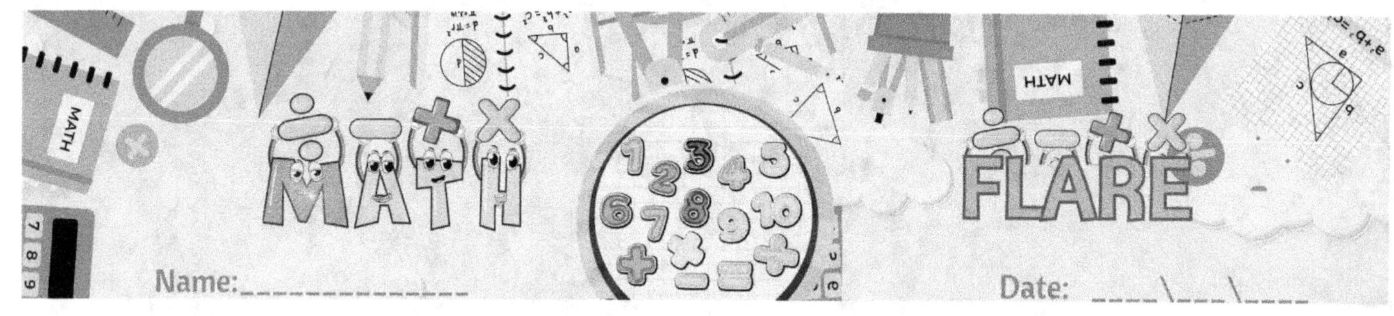

Multi Digit Multiplication

Find the product.

109. 7,952 × 801	110. 9,486 × 947	111. 8,655 × 283
112. 3,082 × 339	113. 6,264 × 840	114. 3,693 × 359
115. 1,404 × 697	116. 3,405 × 183	117. 3,047 × 566

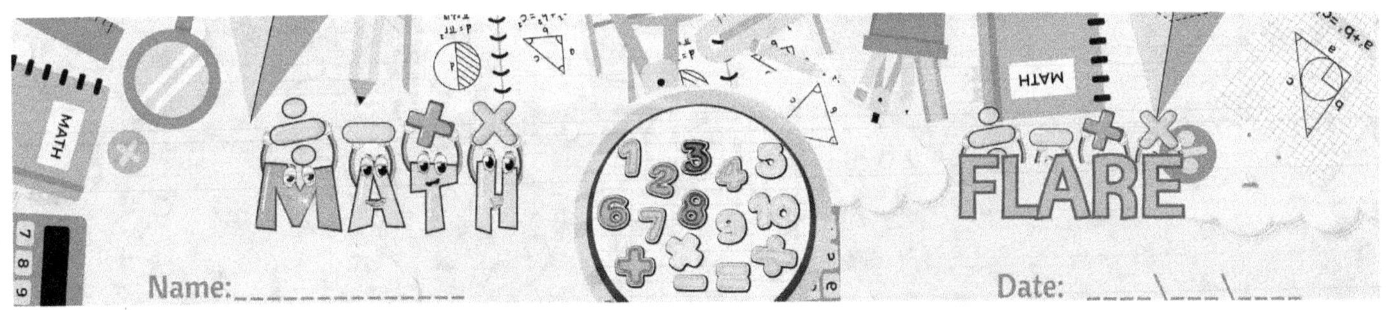

118.
$$9{,}057 \times 355$$

119.
$$1{,}257 \times 771$$

120.
$$1{,}170 \times 276$$

121.
$$3{,}213 \times 415$$

122.
$$6{,}990 \times 337$$

123.
$$8{,}745 \times 431$$

124.
$$1{,}198 \times 965$$

125.
$$2{,}061 \times 111$$

126.
$$5{,}673 \times 349$$

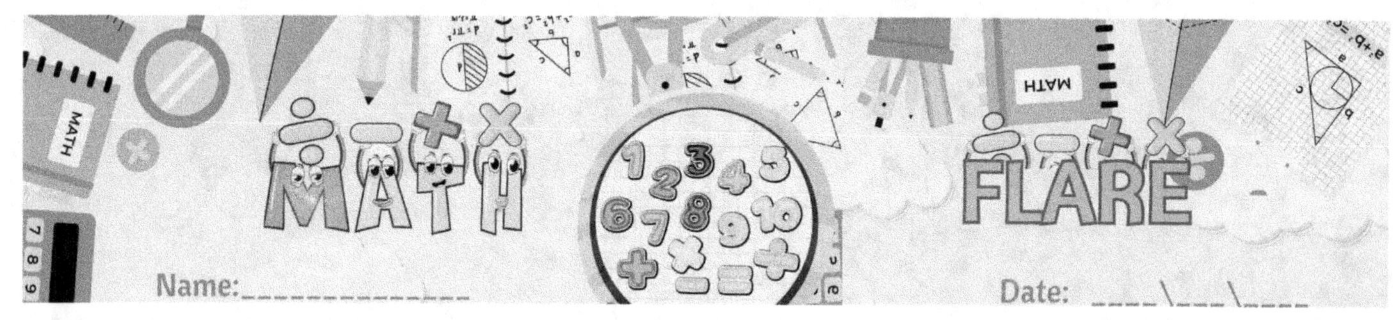

127. 5,440
    ×   317

128. 3,996
    ×   954

129. 6,270
    ×   868

130. 8,218
    ×   424

131. 9,927
    ×   799

132. 9,660
    ×   619

133. 1,482
    ×   662

134. 2,383
    ×   987

135. 5,123
    ×   134

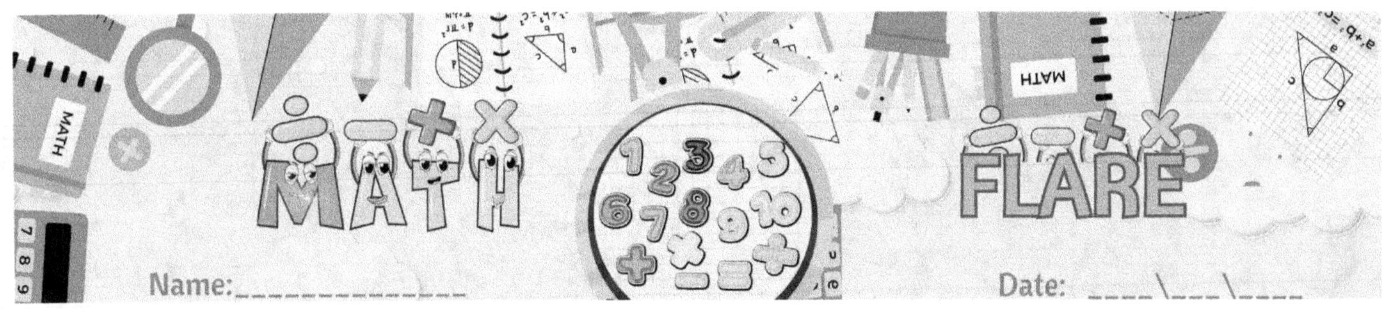

136. 9,384 × 123	137. 7,850 × 772	138. 7,269 × 550
139. 5,843 × 970	140. 4,646 × 295	141. 8,206 × 403
142. 2,533 × 129	143. 2,308 × 991	144. 6,390 × 987

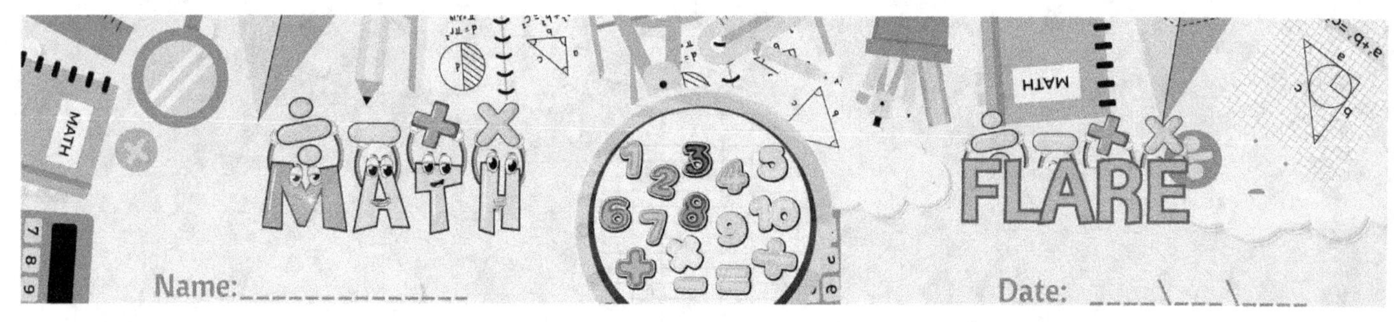

145. 2,667
     × 949

146. 7,279
     × 256

147. 9,500
     × 692

148. 2,835
     × 521

149. 4,492
     × 180

150. 2,890
     × 312

151. 2,933
     × 132

152. 5,539
     × 172

153. 1,725
     × 544

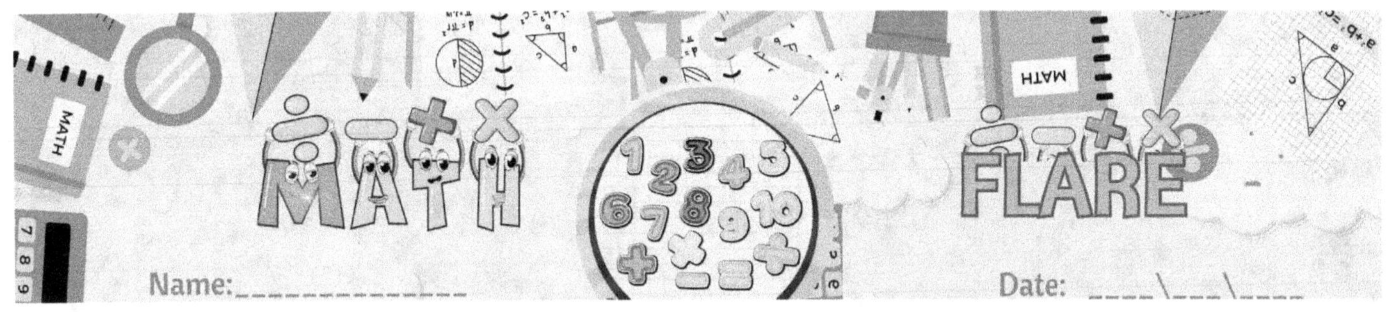

154. 5,637
    × 771

155. 5,899
    × 849

156. 4,709
    × 656

157. 5,044
    × 626

158. 6,041
    × 689

159. 6,463
    × 936

160. 4,885
    × 156

161. 1,234
    × 250

162. 8,210
    × 561

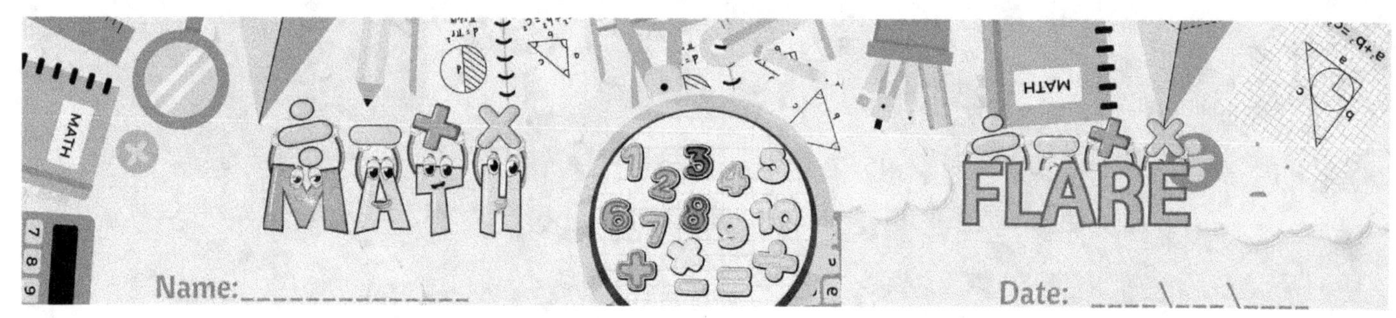

163.   4,060
    ×   781

164.   1,732
    ×   193

165.   5,887
    ×   305

166.   2,011
    ×   504

167.   7,819
    ×   252

168.   1,015
    ×   788

169.   8,489
    ×   181

170.   9,569
    ×   686

171.   5,279
    ×   866

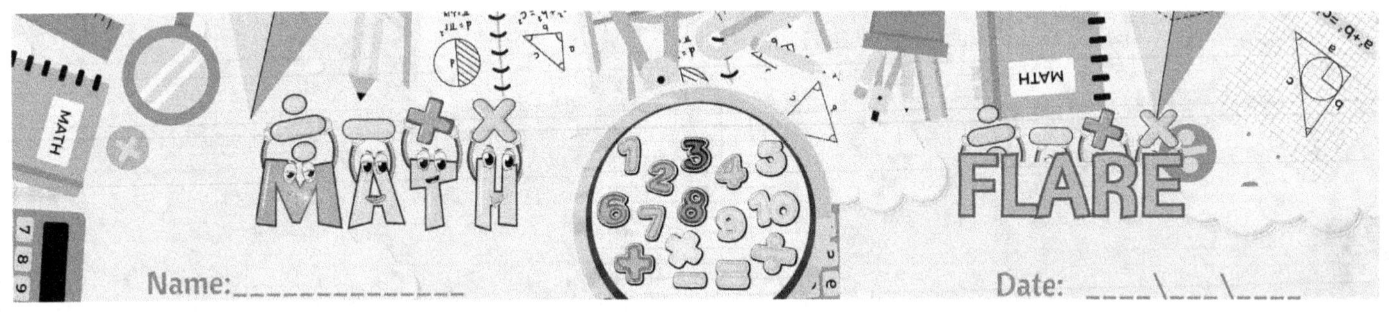

Long Division: Remainders

Find the quotient.

172.

12) 30,189

173.

10) 50,873

174.

7) 14,478

175.

6) 75,513

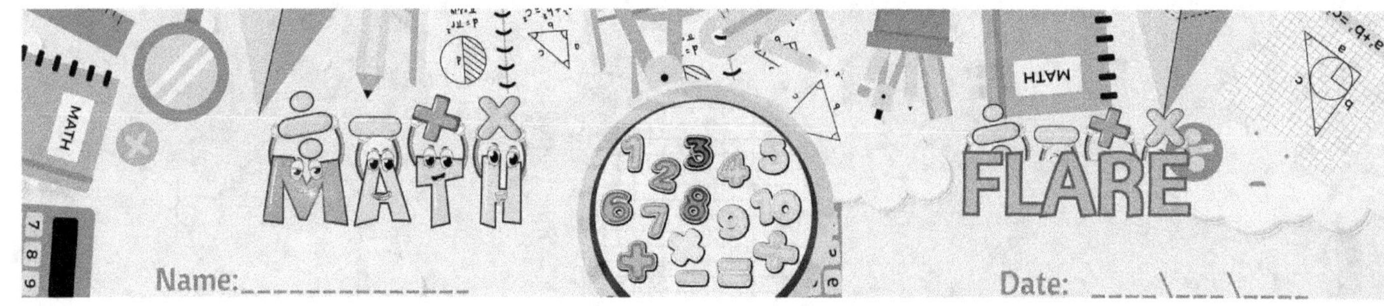

176.

$$6\overline{)39{,}180}$$

177.

$$3\overline{)99{,}293}$$

178.

$$8\overline{)38{,}794}$$

179.

$$2\overline{)61{,}008}$$

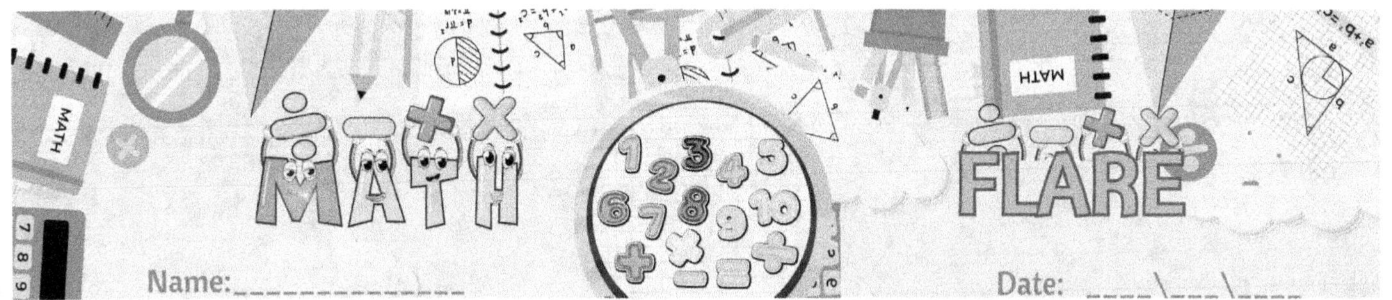

180.

$$14 \overline{)\ 12{,}006}$$

181.

$$10 \overline{)\ 60{,}519}$$

182.

$$12 \overline{)\ 70{,}721}$$

183.

$$4 \overline{)\ 84{,}356}$$

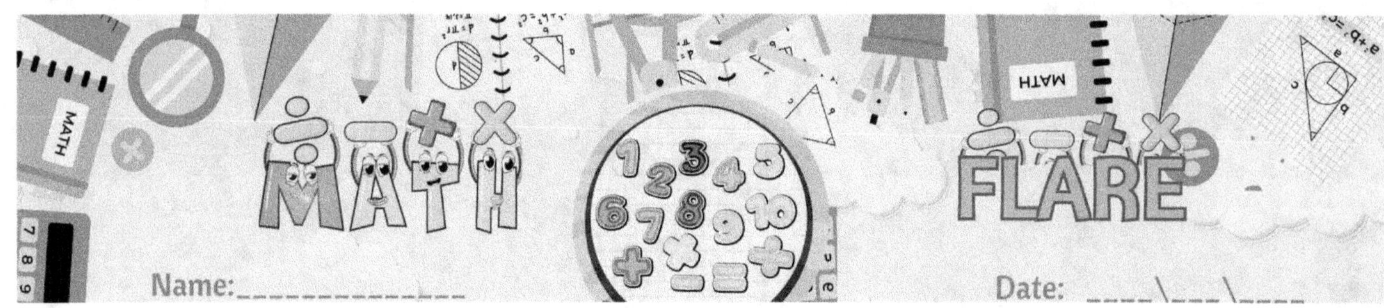

184.

10$\overline{)24{,}720}$

185.

9$\overline{)75{,}962}$

186.

16$\overline{)85{,}541}$

187.

5$\overline{)19{,}629}$

188.

$$9 \overline{)\smash{\,82{,}210}}$$

189.

$$2 \overline{)\smash{\,18{,}115}}$$

190.

$$4 \overline{)\smash{\,18{,}750}}$$

191.

$$11 \overline{)\smash{\,63{,}162}}$$

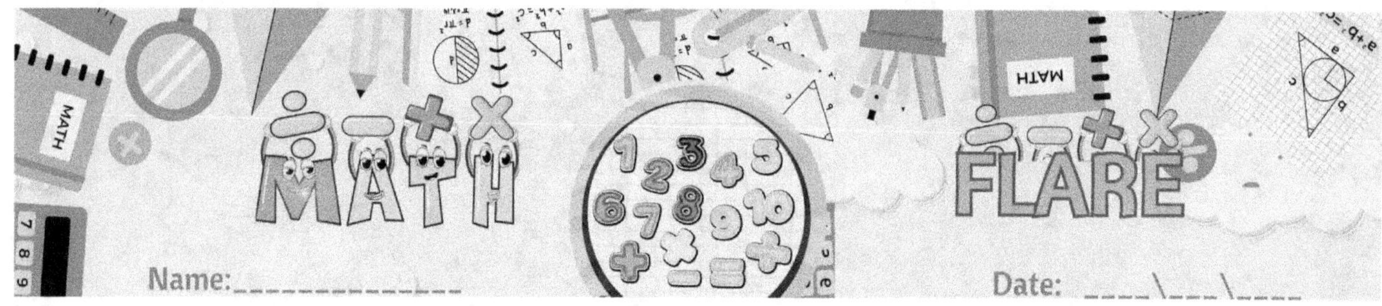

192.

10$\overline{)72{,}256}$

193.

7$\overline{)24{,}869}$

194.

13$\overline{)29{,}672}$

195.

4$\overline{)77{,}329}$

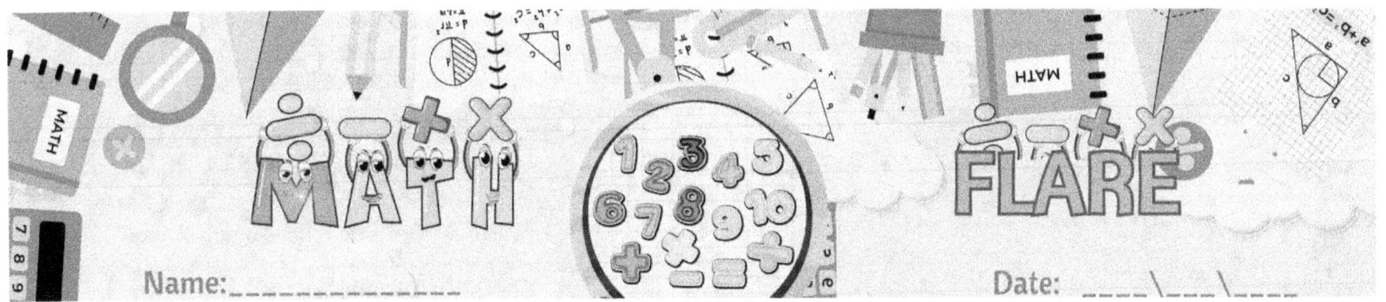

196.

$$9\overline{)88{,}845}$$

197.

$$4\overline{)77{,}465}$$

198.

$$6\overline{)30{,}987}$$

199.

$$14\overline{)10{,}058}$$

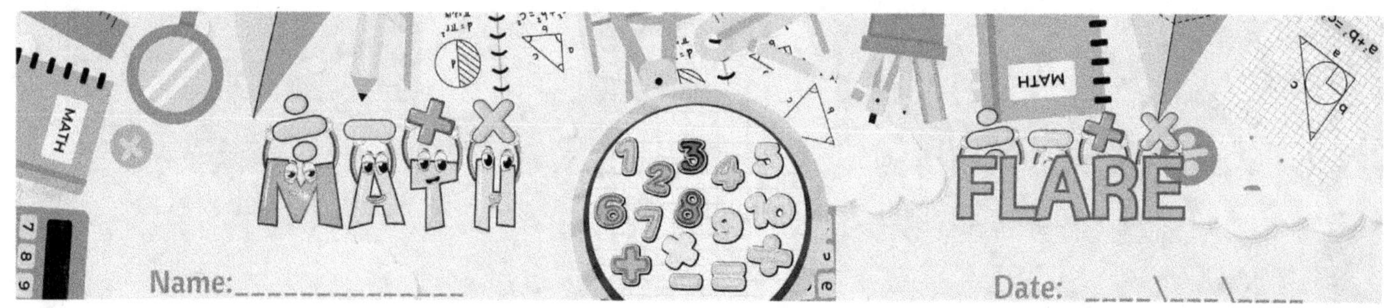

200.

$$8\overline{)76{,}229}$$

201.

$$13\overline{)32{,}917}$$

202.

$$8\overline{)59{,}258}$$

203.

$$12\overline{)43{,}306}$$

204.

$$17 \overline{)\,22{,}045}$$

205.

$$18 \overline{)\,34{,}463}$$

206.

$$12 \overline{)\,31{,}415}$$

207.

$$18 \overline{)\,93{,}640}$$

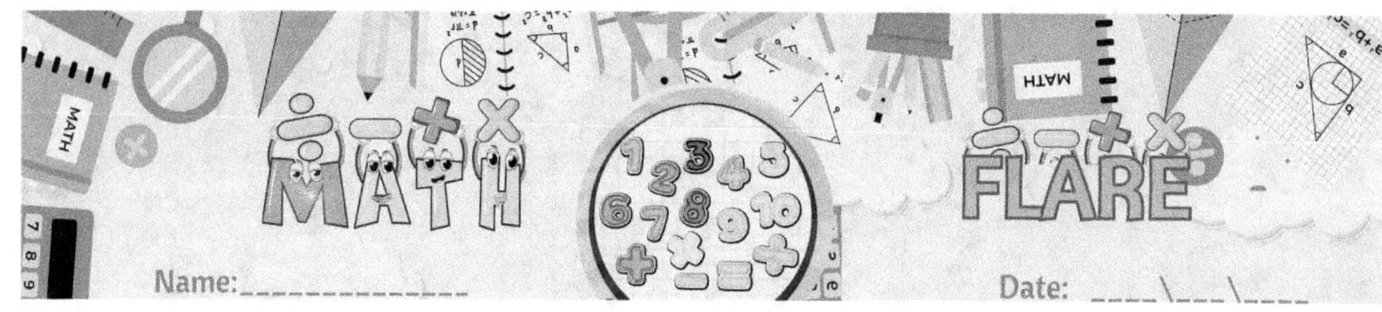

208.

$$3\overline{)14{,}832}$$

209.

$$6\overline{)75{,}321}$$

210.

$$12\overline{)43{,}480}$$

211.

$$12\overline{)92{,}044}$$

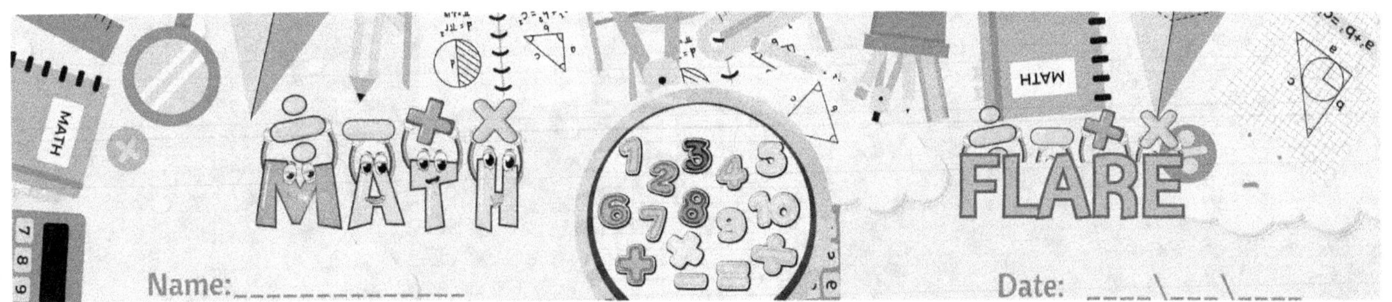

212.

$13\overline{)74{,}602}$

213.

$11\overline{)56{,}145}$

214.

$2\overline{)14{,}125}$

215.

$12\overline{)92{,}500}$

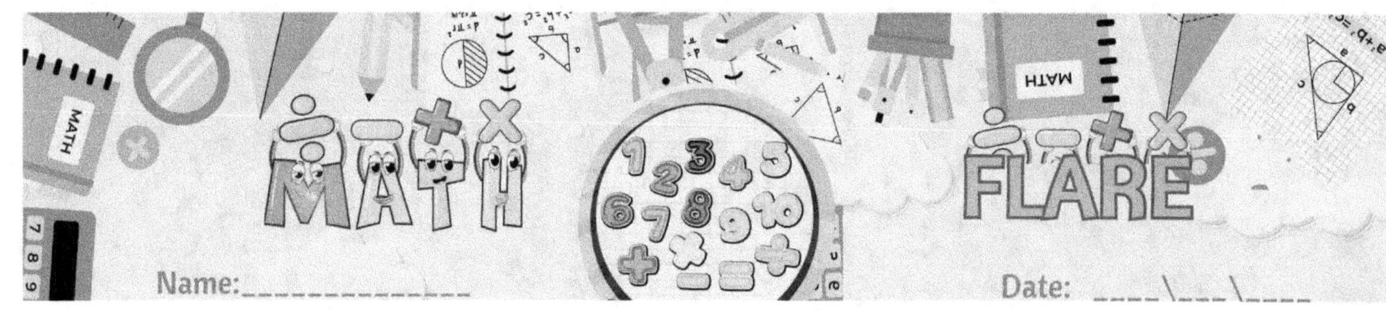

216.

$$9\overline{)47{,}065}$$

217.

$$16\overline{)34{,}180}$$

218.

$$2\overline{)88{,}093}$$

219.

$$8\overline{)97{,}225}$$

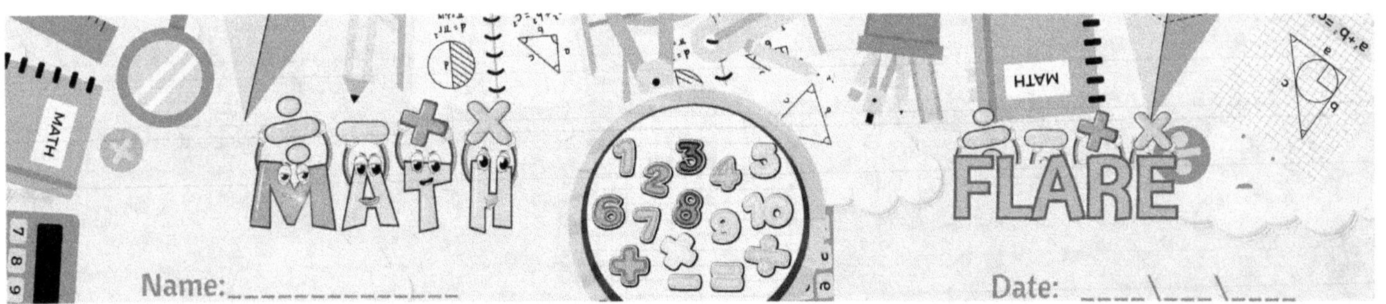

220.

$$13 \overline{)\ 15{,}030}$$

221.

$$9 \overline{)\ 24{,}426}$$

222.

$$17 \overline{)\ 41{,}754}$$

223.

$$8 \overline{)\ 90{,}712}$$

224.

$$17 \overline{)48{,}917}$$

225.

$$5 \overline{)13{,}668}$$

226.

$$16 \overline{)56{,}571}$$

227.

$$6 \overline{)38{,}359}$$

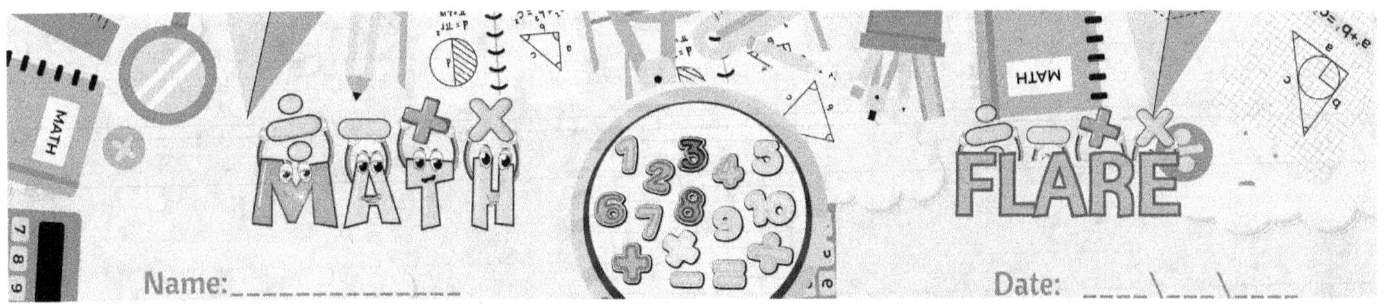

228.

$$15\overline{)47{,}111}$$

229.

$$19\overline{)87{,}941}$$

230.

$$18\overline{)84{,}376}$$

231.

$$4\overline{)53{,}464}$$

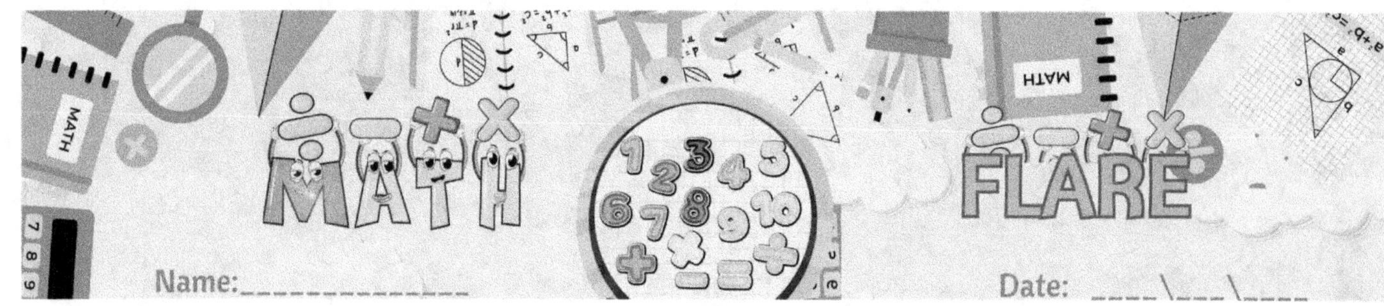

232.

$$15\overline{)93{,}305}$$

233.

$$17\overline{)54{,}605}$$

234.

$$5\overline{)36{,}419}$$

235.

$$3\overline{)12{,}900}$$

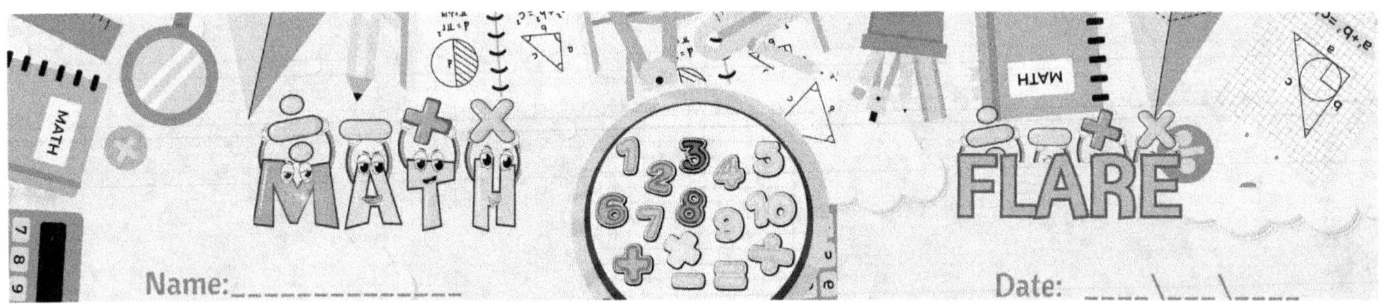

236.

$$9 \overline{\smash{)}16{,}810}$$

237.

$$15 \overline{\smash{)}27{,}355}$$

238.

$$12 \overline{\smash{)}43{,}459}$$

239.

$$18 \overline{\smash{)}26{,}749}$$

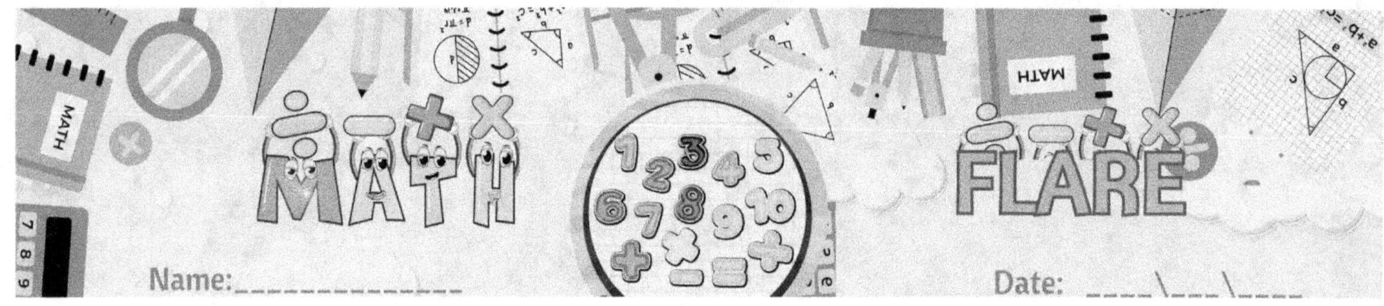

240.

$$6 \overline{)73,120}$$

241.

$$6 \overline{)14,067}$$

242.

$$15 \overline{)97,461}$$

243.

$$14 \overline{)13,745}$$

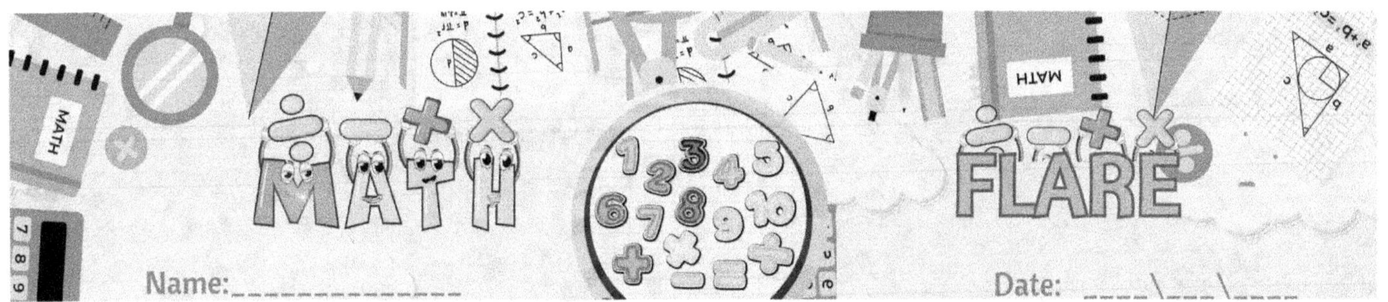

244.

$$3\overline{)17{,}916}$$

245.

$$5\overline{)42{,}482}$$

246.

$$2\overline{)22{,}675}$$

247.

$$5\overline{)57{,}357}$$

248.

$$3 \overline{)23{,}815}$$

249.

$$14 \overline{)50{,}559}$$

250.

$$3 \overline{)41{,}052}$$

251.

$$7 \overline{)11{,}828}$$

Name:_________________   Date: ____________

Using the Power of 10

252.   1,000
     × 1,000

253.   6,000
     × 1,000

254.
     100⟌4,000

255.   5,000
     ×   0.1

256.
     10⟌5,000

257.   1,000
     ×   100

258.   3,000
     ×   0.1

259.   6,000
     ×   0.1

260.   8,000
     ×   0.1

261.
     100⟌4,000

262.   5,000
     × 1,000

263.   3,000
     ×   10

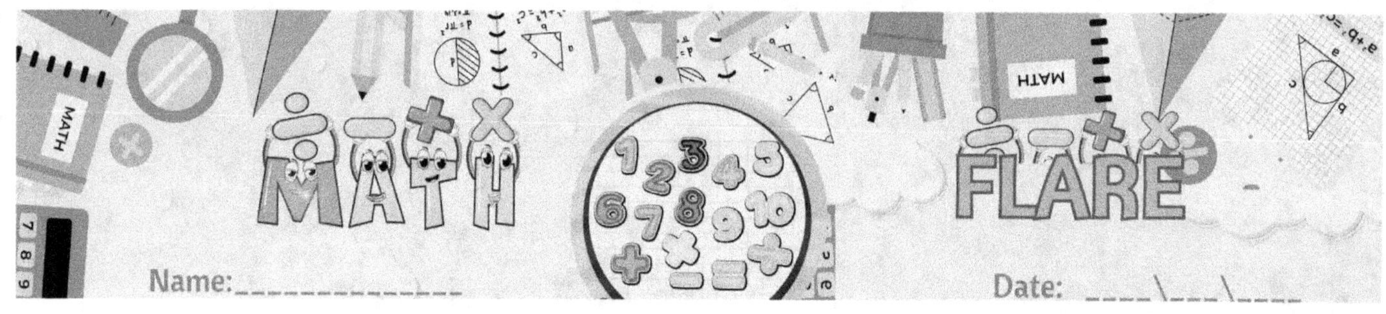

264. $1{,}000\overline{)8{,}000}$

265. $10\overline{)1{,}000}$

266.
$$\begin{array}{r} 2{,}000 \\ \times\quad 0.1 \\ \hline \end{array}$$

267.
$$\begin{array}{r} 1{,}000 \\ \times\ 1{,}000 \\ \hline \end{array}$$

268.
$$\begin{array}{r} 5{,}000 \\ \times\quad 0.1 \\ \hline \end{array}$$

269.
$$\begin{array}{r} 7{,}000 \\ \times\quad 10 \\ \hline \end{array}$$

270. $100\overline{)7{,}000}$

271. $1{,}000\overline{)7{,}000}$

272. $100\overline{)3{,}000}$

273. $10\overline{)9{,}000}$

274. $10\overline{)4{,}000}$

275.
$$\begin{array}{r} 5{,}000 \\ \times\quad 0.1 \\ \hline \end{array}$$

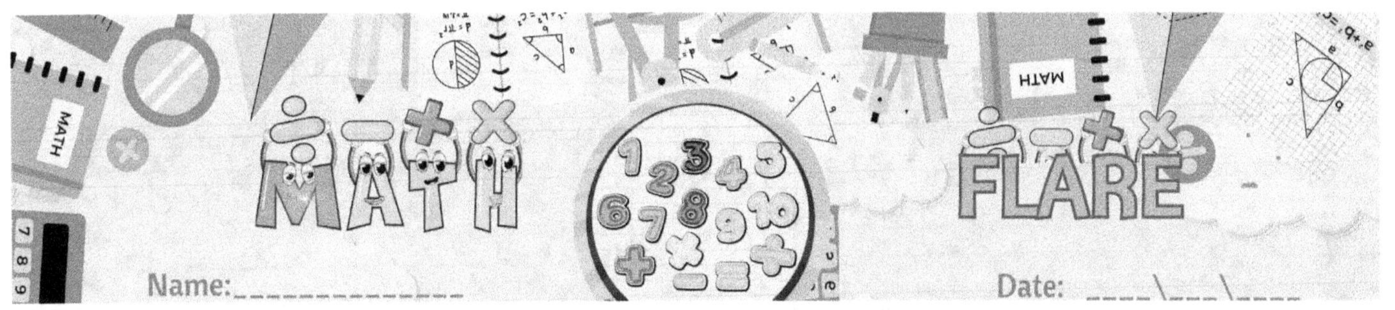

276.
$$6{,}000 \times 100$$

277.
$$9{,}000 \times 1{,}000$$

278.
$$1{,}000 \overline{)\,4{,}000}$$

279.
$$8{,}000 \times 10$$

280.
$$3{,}000 \times 100$$

281.
$$1{,}000 \times 100$$

282.
$$10 \overline{)\,1{,}000}$$

283.
$$3{,}000 \times 1{,}000$$

284.
$$10 \overline{)\,3{,}000}$$

285.
$$5{,}000 \times 1{,}000$$

286.
$$100 \overline{)\,4{,}000}$$

287.
$$6{,}000 \times 1{,}000$$

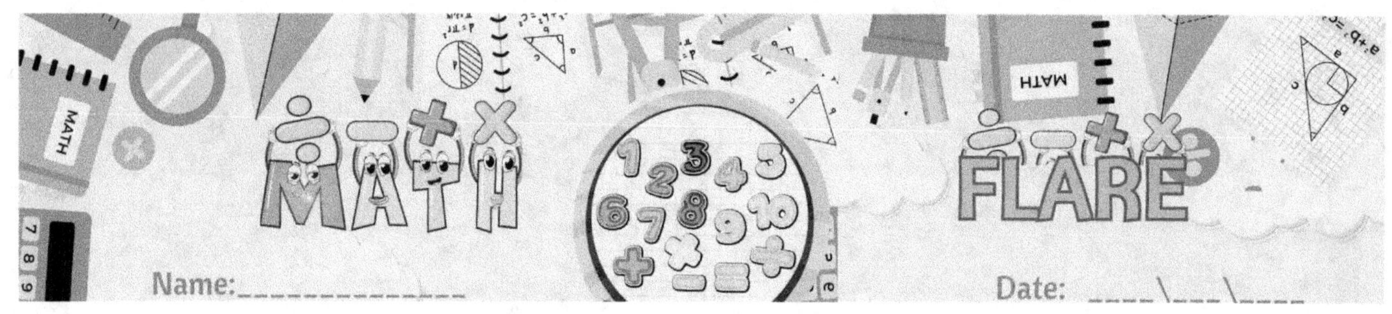

288.
$$9{,}000 \times 0.1$$

289.
$$1{,}000 \overline{)1{,}000}$$

290.
$$0.1 \overline{)6{,}000}$$

291.
$$1{,}000 \overline{)7{,}000}$$

292.
$$10 \overline{)3{,}000}$$

293.
$$0.1 \overline{)2{,}000}$$

294.
$$1{,}000 \overline{)4{,}000}$$

295.
$$0.1 \overline{)4{,}000}$$

296.
$$7{,}000 \times 1{,}000$$

297.
$$4{,}000 \times 1{,}000$$

298.
$$0.1 \overline{)9{,}000}$$

299.
$$2{,}000 \times 10$$

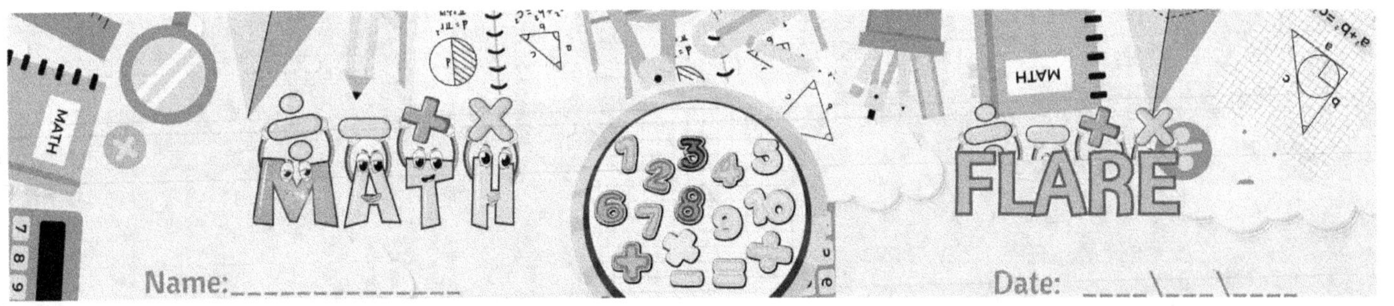

300.

$$100 \overline{)1{,}000}$$

301.

$$10 \overline{)8{,}000}$$

302.

$$1{,}000 \overline{)9{,}000}$$

303.

$$100 \overline{)7{,}000}$$

304.

$$\begin{array}{r} 8{,}000 \\ \times \quad 10 \\ \hline \end{array}$$

305.

$$\begin{array}{r} 7{,}000 \\ \times \quad 100 \\ \hline \end{array}$$

306.

$$1{,}000 \overline{)4{,}000}$$

307.

$$100 \overline{)1{,}000}$$

308.

$$\begin{array}{r} 2{,}000 \\ \times \quad 100 \\ \hline \end{array}$$

309.

$$10 \overline{)8{,}000}$$

310.

$$10 \overline{)9{,}000}$$

311.

$$\begin{array}{r} 6{,}000 \\ \times \quad 100 \\ \hline \end{array}$$

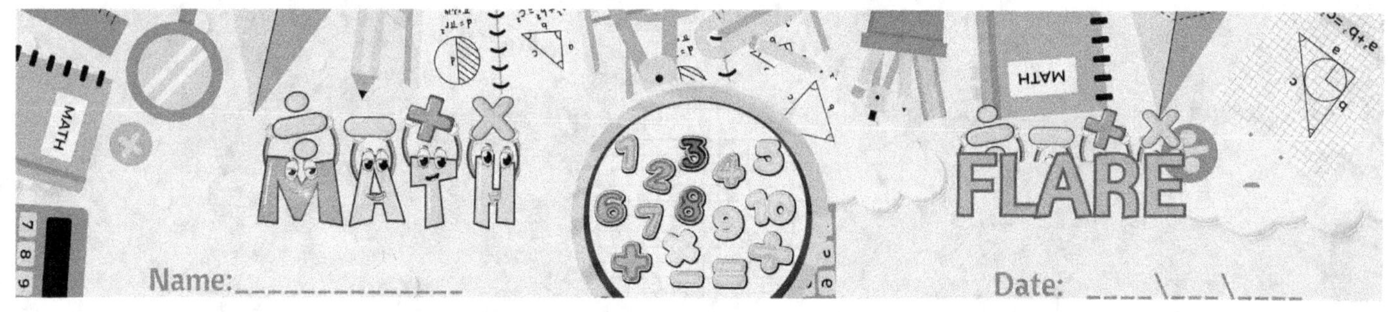

Multiplication Word Problems

312. Diego can solve six math problems in one hour. How many problems can Diego solve in 16 hours?

313. Josiah can lift 10 pounds of weight. How many pounds of weight can he lift in 14 repetitions?

314. Arianna has 10 books on each shelf, and there are four shelves. How many books does Arianna have in total?

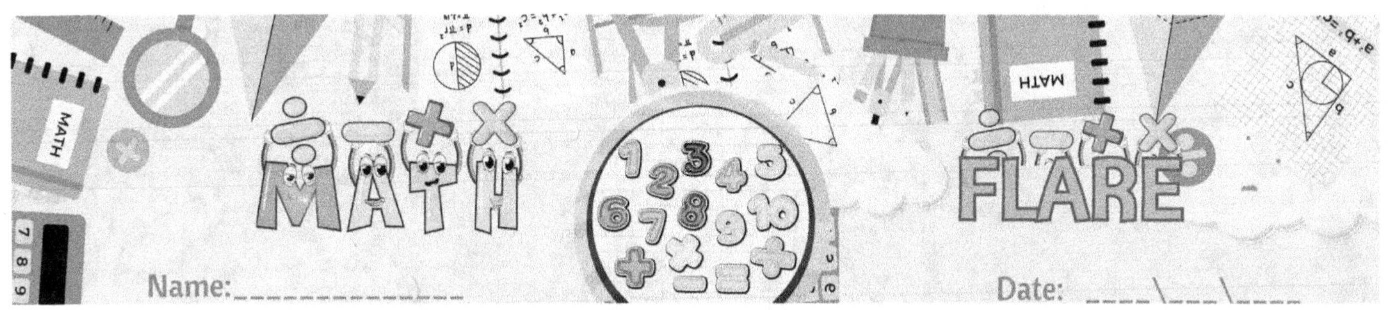

315. Harper has 16 vases of flowers. Each vase has 19 flowers. How many flowers does Harper have in all?

316. There are eight flowers in each bouquet. If Riley has 14 bouquets, how many flowers does Riley have in all?

317. Christopher can ride 20 miles in one hour. How far can he ride in six hours?

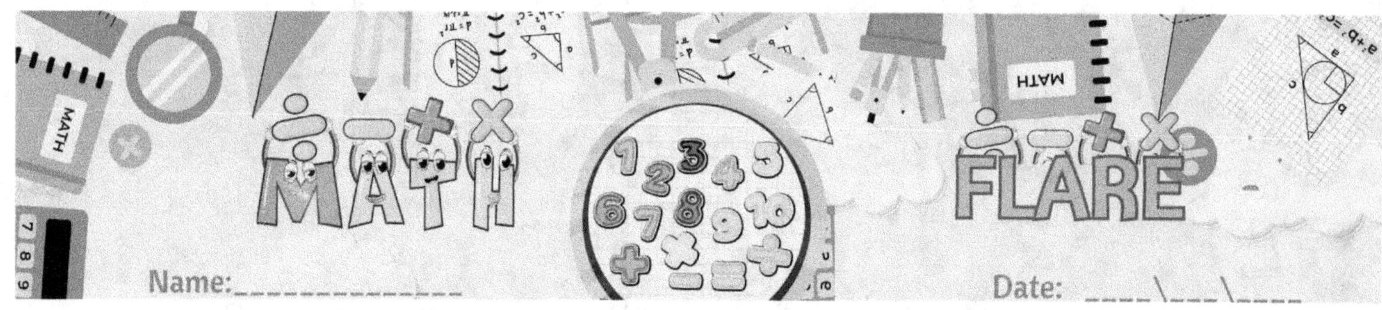

318. There are 20 bananas in each bunch. If Paisley buys 17 bunches, how many bananas will Paisley have?

319. Matthew sells seven cakes each day at his bakery. If he works three days, how many cakes does he sell?

320. If a train travels at seven miles per hour for 19 hours, how far will it go?

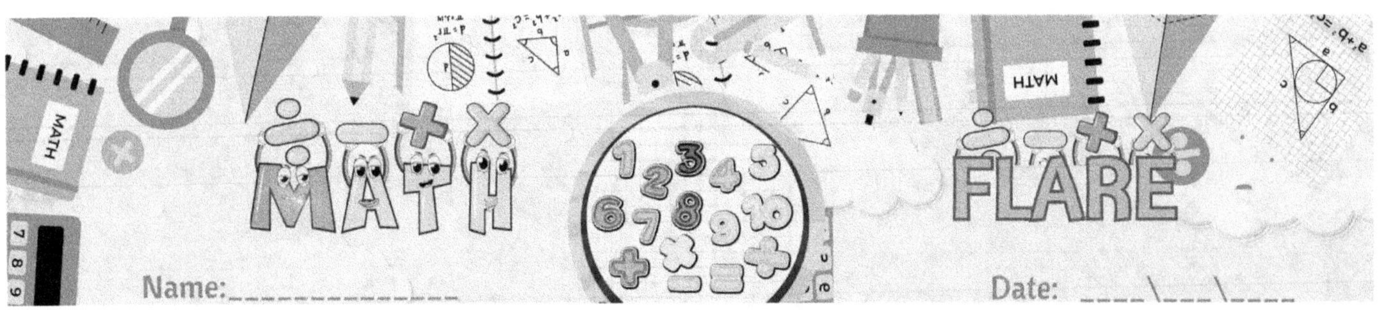

321. Elijah can lift 19 pounds of weight. How many pounds of weight can Elijah lift in total if he lifts for 17 sets?

322. Benjamin runs two miles every day. How many miles will Benjamin run in 14 days?

323. Claire has five jars of jam. Each jar has 12 ounces of jam. How many ounces of jam does Claire have in all?

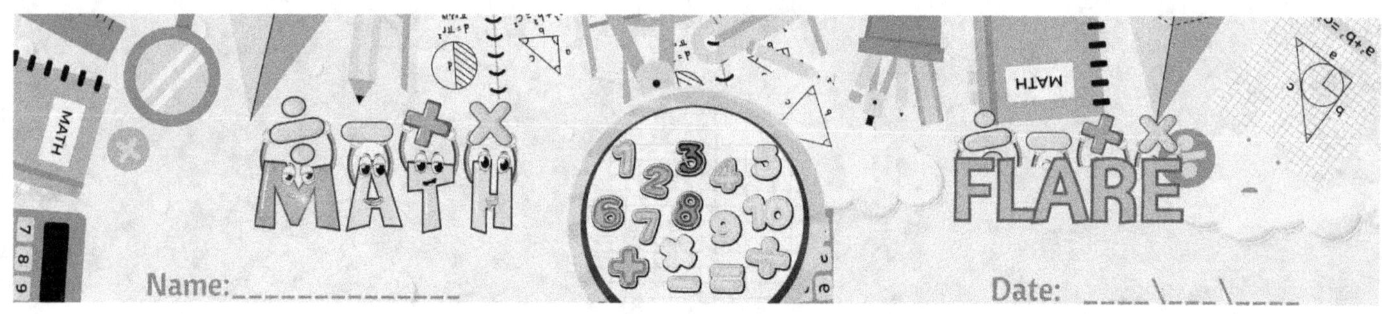

324. Molly baked six batches of cookies. Each batch had 10 cookies. How many cookies did Molly bake in all?

325. There are 16 students in a class. If each student needs 10 pencils, how many pencils are needed for the class in total?

326. If a bicycle travels at 17 miles per hour for two hours, how far will it go?

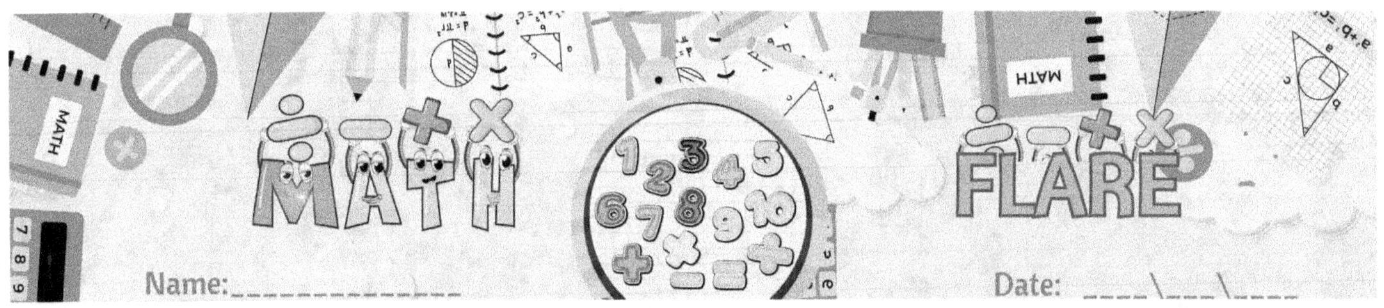

327. There are four pages in a book. If five books are needed for a class, how many pages are there in total?

328. There are 13 thermometers in each bag. If Scarlett buys 16 bags, how many thermometers will Scarlett have?

329. There are 17 shelves in Dylan's bookcase. 20 books can fit on each shelf. How many books can the bookcase hold in total?

330. Gemma wants to make 16 pizzas, and each pizza requires nine cups of cheese. How many cups of cheese does Gemma have?

331. A bookshelf can hold nine books. If there are 18 bookshelves in a room, how many books can the room hold in total?

332. Gabriella has 14 yards of fabric, and each dress requires 15 yards of fabric. How many dresses can Gabriella make?

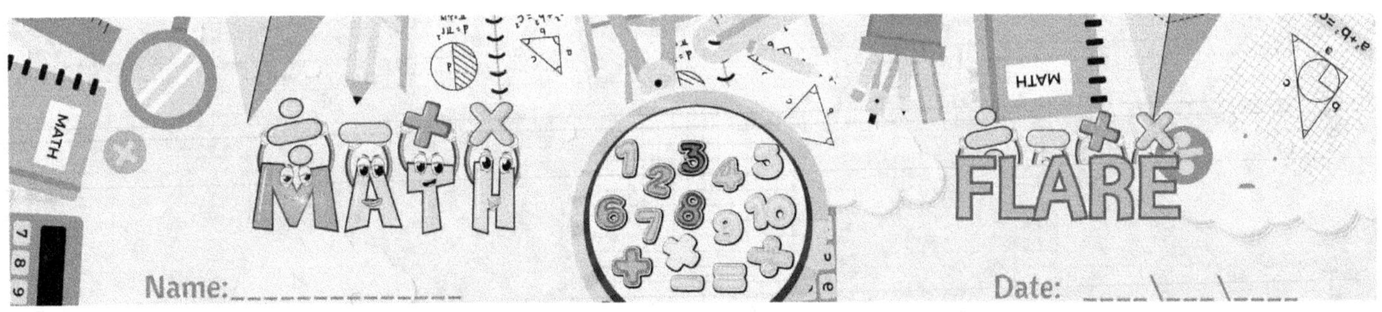

333. A recipe for a cake calls for 11 cups of flour. How many cups of flour are needed to make 12 cakes?

334. There are 12 shelves in a library. Six books can fit on each shelf. How many books the library have in total?

335. If a boat travels at 17 miles per hour for 17 hours, how far will it go?

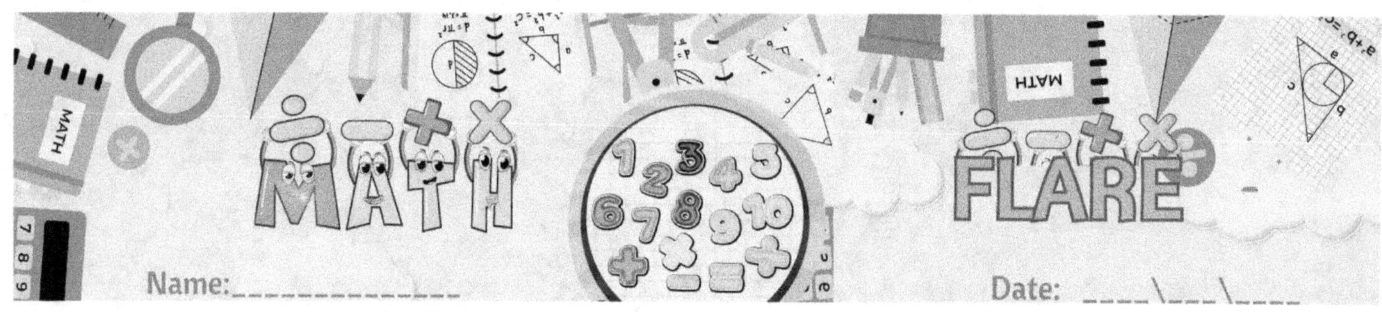

336. A movie theater can seat 11 people. How many people can it seat in seven showings?

337. A box contains eight bottles of juice, and each bottle contains 17 ounces of juice. How many ounces of juice are there in total?

338. There are 18 cars in a parking lot. If each car needs 19 liters of gasoline, how many liters of gasoline are needed for all the cars?

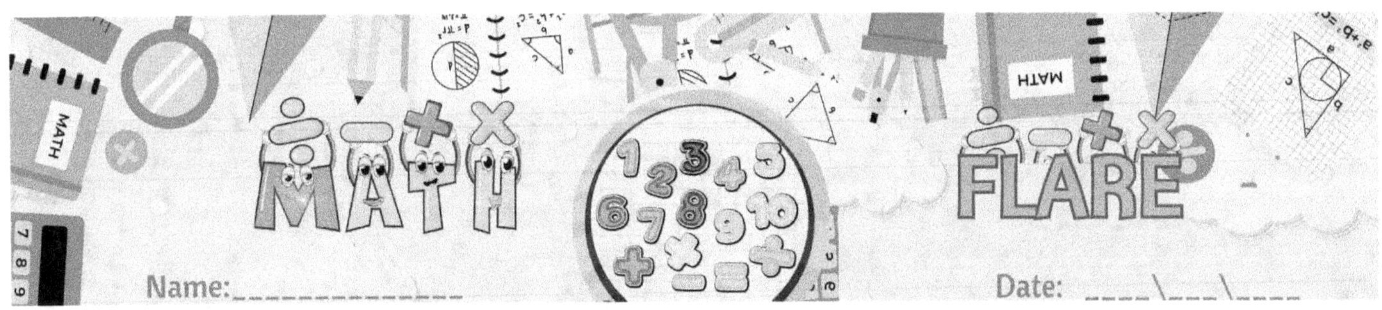

339. Lily wants to make 11 flower arrangements, and each arrangement requires 13 flowers. How many flowers does Lily need in total?

340. If there are 13 students in each classroom and there are 18 classrooms, how many students are there in total?

341. Ellie has nine boxes of chocolates. Each box has two chocolates. How many chocolates does Ellie have in all?

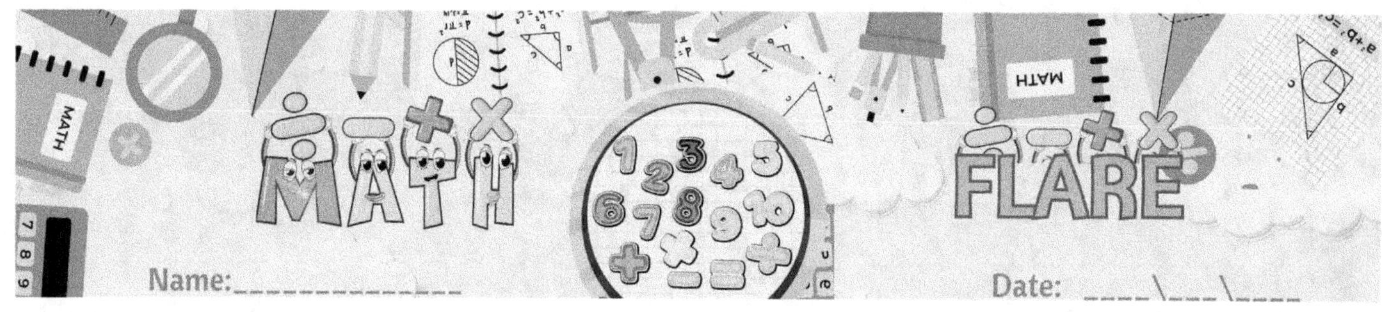

Division Word Problems

342. If a garden is 272 feet long and it is divided into eight equal parts, how long is each part?

343. How many three cm pieces of pipe can you cut from a pipe that is 96 cm long?

344. Joseph drove 936 miles in 12 hours. What was Joseph's average speed in miles per hour?

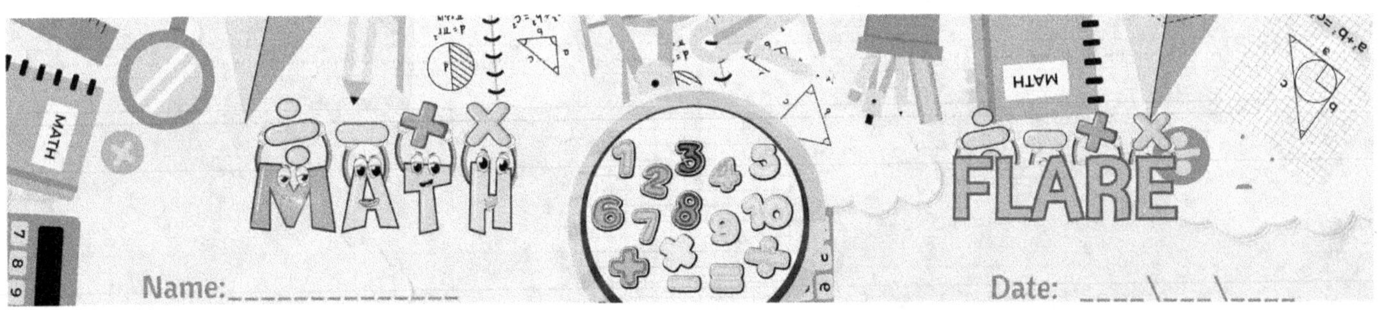

345. Avery has 336 thermometers and wants to divide them equally among 14 people. How many thermometers will each person get?

346. Cameron has 66 pages of homework to do. If he wants to finish his homework in two days, how many pages does he need to do each day?

347. Ella can run 720 miles in eight hours. How many miles can she run in 1 hour?

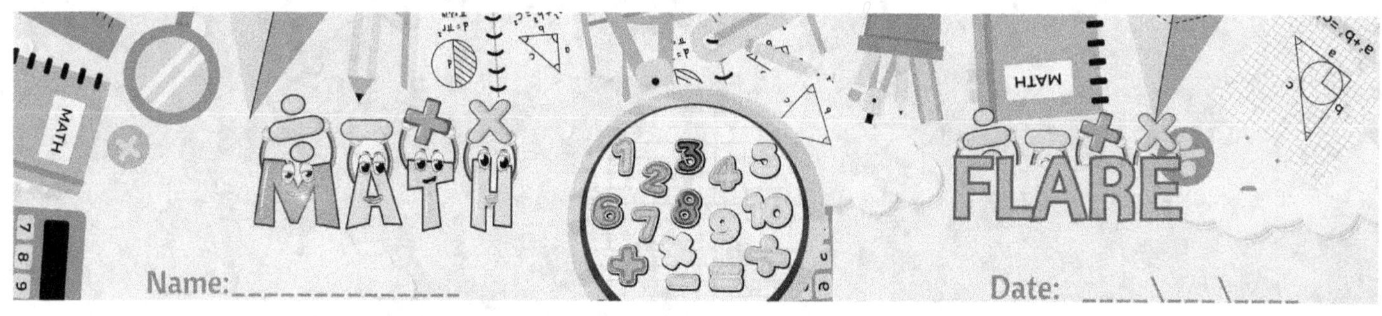

348. Brody has 88 dollars and wants to buy 11 desks. How much can he spend on each desks?

349. A box contains 175 candy bars. If each candy bar has five calories, how many calories are there in the box?

350. At a restaurant, five friends decided to divide the bill equally. If each person paid $65, then what was the total bill?

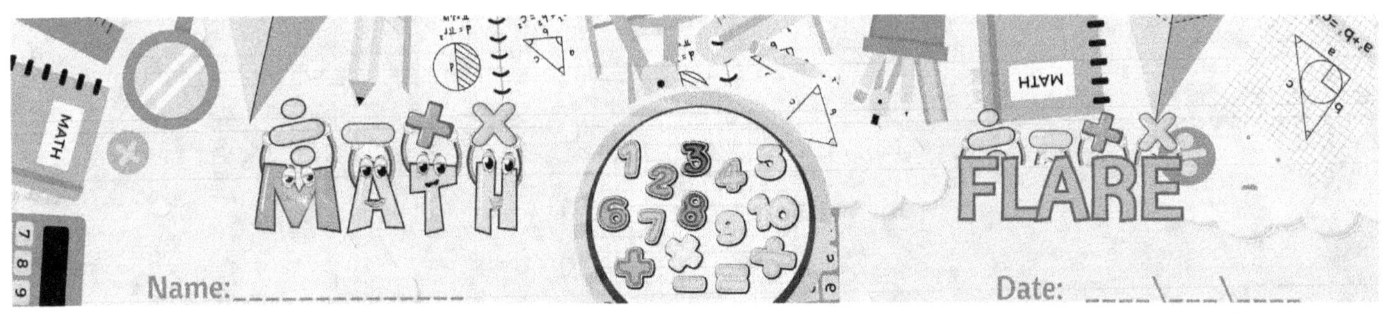

351. Hazel is filling up water bottles. Each bottle holds 20 ounces of water. If Hazel has 100 ounces of water, how many water bottles can she fill up?

352. Serenity has 1,248 gloves and wants to divide them equally among 13 children. How many gloves will each child get?

353. A pool is 1,083 meters long. If it is divided into 19 equal parts, how long is each part?

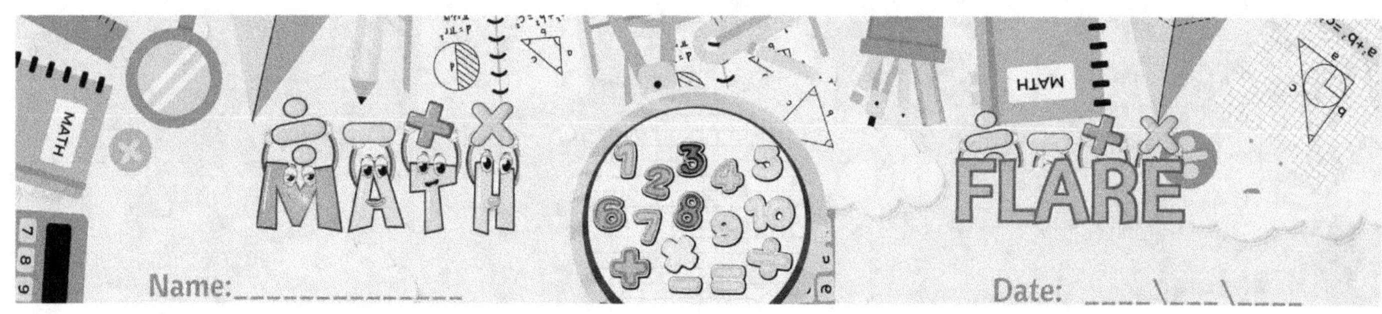

354. Lincoln is reading a book with 540 pages. If Lincoln wants to read the same number of pages every day, how many pages would Lincoln have to read each day to finish in 15 days?

355. Audrey made 469 cookies for a bake sale. She put the cookies in bags, with seven cookies in each bag. How many bags did she have for the bake sale?

356. A roll of tape is 156 feet long. If Caroline needs to cut the tape into six pieces that are all the same length, how long will each piece be?

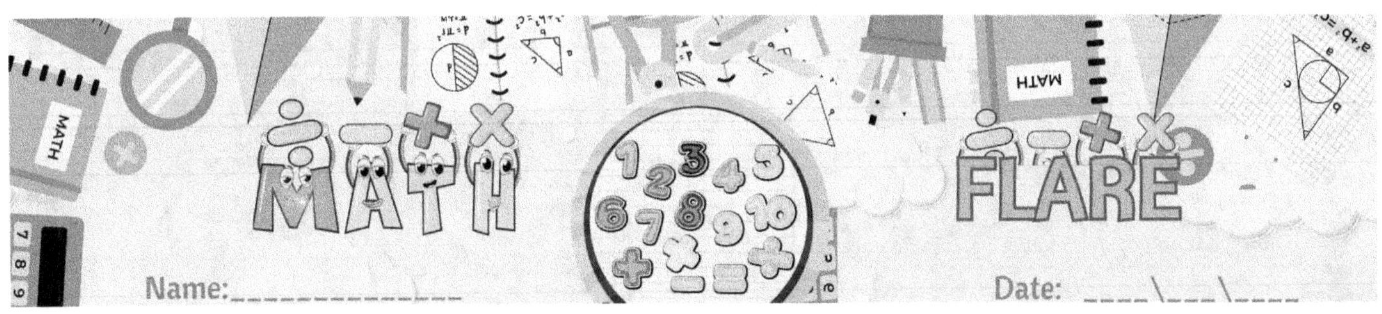

357. Savannah has 810 knives. If Savannah divides them evenly among nine children, how many knives will each child get?

358. If a field is 84 acres and it is divided into two equal parts, how many acres is each part?

359. If Ryder has 385 radios and wants to share them equally among 11 friends, how many radios will each friend get?

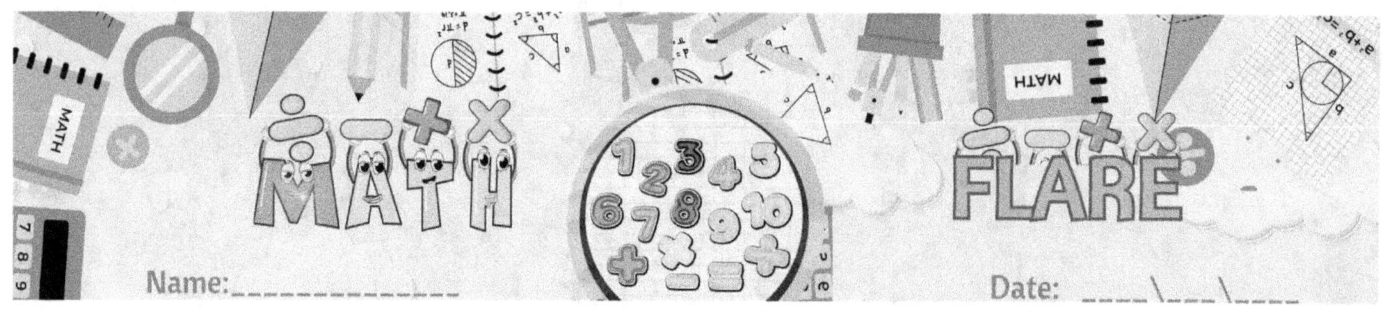

360. Zoey bought 13 combs for a total of $260. How much did each combs cost?

361. Emilia is packing 162 cupcakes into boxes. Each box can hold two cupcakes. How many boxes will Emilia need?

362. If Penelope has 720 cameras and wants to distribute them equally to 12 students, how many cameras will each student get?

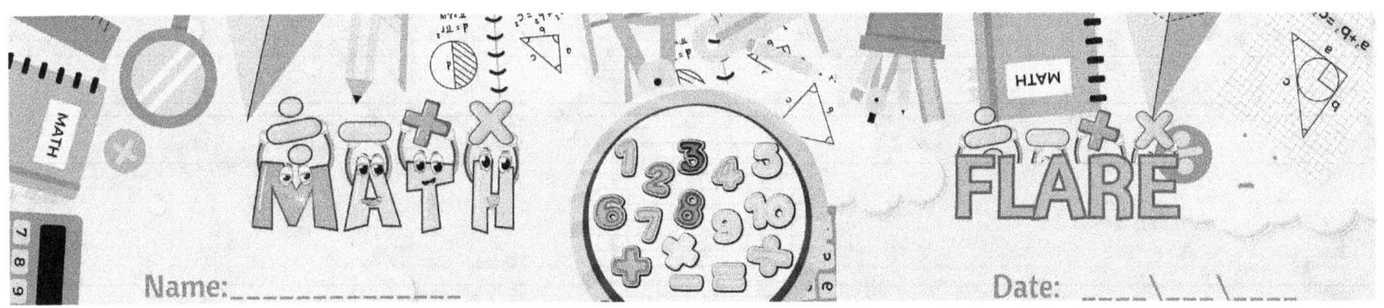

Name:________________   Date: _______________

363. It takes Kaylee 18 minutes to write 1 page. How many
     pages can Kaylee write in 306 minutes?

364. A recipe calls for 855 cups of sugar to make 19 cookies.
     How much sugar is needed to make 1 cookie?

365. Aurora has 574 cookies and wants to divide them equally
     into seven bags. How many cookies will be in each bag?

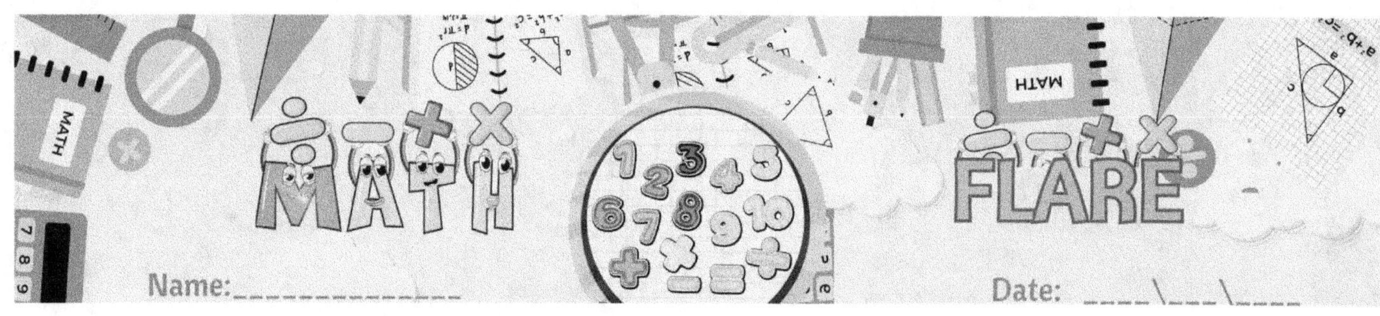

366. You have 288 hats and want to share them equally with 16 people. How many hats would each person get?

367. A book has 970 chapters. If you want to read the book in 10 days, how many chapters do you need to read per day?

368. A car can travel 684 miles on 18 gallons of gas. How many miles can it travel on 1 gallon of gas?

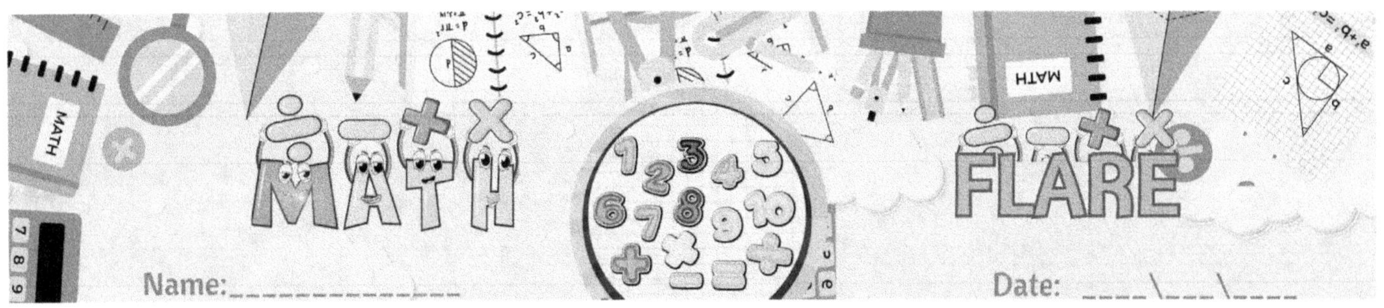

369. If a garden is 360 feet wide and it is divided into nine equal parts, how wide is each part?

370. How many nine cm pieces of rope can you cut from a rope that is 486 cm long?

371. A box of chocolates weighs 247 pounds. If one chocolate weighs 13 pounds, how many chocolates are there in the box?

ANSWERS

Page 1: Multiplication (3 Digit)

1. 137,592	2. 267,344	3. 329,476	4. 199,716
5. 253,095	6. 297,336	7. 85,920	8. 413,082
9. 110,843	10. 120,032	11. 67,467	12. 398,970
13. 142,233	14. 447,426	15. 213,689	16. 217,165
17. 159,095	18. 40,869	19. 757,881	20. 523,778
21. 109,335	22. 297,387	23. 162,864	24. 156,723
25. 341,649	26. 283,917	27. 83,619	28. 160,633
29. 248,865	30. 33,507	31. 162,565	32. 297,066
33. 42,218	34. 120,360	35. 137,735	36. 360,661
37. 211,328	38. 360,327	39. 283,605	40. 162,134
41. 34,320	42. 56,202	43. 359,199	44. 563,101
45. 802,128	46. 377,897	47. 426,184	48. 207,318
49. 93,473	50. 44,619	51. 456,976	52. 275,650
53. 71,700	54. 585,610	55. 355,743	56. 185,514
57. 98,000	58. 154,512	59. 252,229	60. 45,171
61. 193,830	62. 158,792	63. 290,697	64. 175,538
65. 345,948	66. 86,136	67. 59,364	68. 493,667
69. 566,214	70. 151,202	71. 37,530	72. 434,226
73. 152,776	74. 646,923	75. 433,671	76. 743,895

77. 33,916	78. 218,280	79. 232,232	80. 221,298
81. 181,170	82. 478,721	83. 94,423	84. 166,600
85. 344,058	86. 270,342	87. 87,464	88. 375,360
89. 269,675	90. 105,264	91. 44,460	92. 62,040
93. 204,440	94. 386,552	95. 387,500	96. 444,276
97. 190,080	98. 352,588	99. 74,292	100. 70,225
101. 199,326	102. 93,184	103. 95,930	104. 17,013
105. 122,996	106. 330,035	107. 231,572	108. 374,607

Page 10: Multi Digit Multiplication

109. 6,369,552	110. 8,983,242	111. 2,449,365	112. 1,044,798
113. 5,261,760	114. 1,325,787	115. 978,588	116. 623,115
117. 1,724,602	118. 3,215,235	119. 969,147	120. 322,920
121. 1,333,395	122. 2,355,630	123. 3,769,095	124. 1,156,070
125. 228,771	126. 1,979,877	127. 1,724,480	128. 3,812,184
129. 5,442,360	130. 3,484,432	131. 7,931,673	132. 5,979,540
133. 981,084	134. 2,352,021	135. 686,482	136. 1,154,232
137. 6,060,200	138. 3,997,950	139. 5,667,710	140. 1,370,570
141. 3,307,018	142. 326,757	143. 2,287,228	144. 6,306,930
145. 2,530,983	146. 1,863,424	147. 6,574,000	148. 1,477,035
149. 808,560	150. 901,680	151. 387,156	152. 952,708
153. 938,400	154. 4,346,127	155. 5,008,251	156. 3,089,104

157. 3,157,544   158. 4,162,249   159. 6,049,368   160. 762,060

161. 308,500   162. 4,605,810   163. 3,170,860   164. 334,276

165. 1,795,535   166. 1,013,544   167. 1,970,388   168. 799,820

169. 1,536,509   170. 6,564,334   171. 4,571,614

Page 17:   Long Division: Remainders

172. 2,515 R9   173. 5,087 R3   174. 2,068 R2   175. 12,585 R3

176. 6,530 R0   177. 33,097 R2   178. 4,849 R2   179. 30,504 R0

180. 857 R8   181. 6,051 R9   182. 5,893 R5   183. 21,089 R0

184. 2,472 R0   185. 8,440 R2   186. 5,346 R5   187. 3,925 R4

188. 9,134 R4   189. 9,057 R1   190. 4,687 R2   191. 5,742 R0

192. 7,225 R6   193. 3,552 R5   194. 2,282 R6   195. 19,332 R1

196. 9,871 R6   197. 19,366 R1   198. 5,164 R3   199. 718 R6

200. 9,528 R5   201. 2,532 R1   202. 7,407 R2   203. 3,608 R10

204. 1,296 R13   205. 1,914 R11   206. 2,617 R11   207. 5,202 R4

208. 4,944 R0   209. 12,553 R3   210. 3,623 R4   211. 7,670 R4

212. 5,738 R8   213. 5,104 R1   214. 7,062 R1   215. 7,708 R4

216. 5,229 R4   217. 2,136 R4   218. 44,046 R1   219. 12,153 R1

220. 1,156 R2   221. 2,714 R0   222. 2,456 R2   223. 11,339 R0

224. 2,877 R8   225. 2,733 R3   226. 3,535 R11   227. 6,393 R1

228. 3,140 R11   229. 4,628 R9   230. 4,687 R10   231. 13,366 R0

232. 6,220 R5   233. 3,212 R1   234. 7,283 R4   235. 4,300 R0

236. 1,867 R7   237. 1,823 R10   238. 3,621 R7   239. 1,486 R1

240. 12,186 R4   241. 2,344 R3   242. 6,497 R6   243. 981 R11

244. 5,972 R0   245. 8,496 R2   246. 11,337 R1   247. 11,471 R2

248. 7,938 R1   249. 3,611 R5   250. 13,684 R0   251. 1,689 R5

Page 37: Using the Power of 10

252. 1,000,000   253. 6,000,000   254. 40   255. 500.0

256. 500   257. 100,000   258. 300.0   259. 600.0

260. 800.0   261. 40   262. 5,000,000   263. 30,000

264. 8   265. 100   266. 200.0   267. 1,000,000

268. 500.0   269. 70,000   270. 70   271. 7

272. 30   273. 900   274. 400   275. 500.0

276. 600,000   277. 9,000,000   278. 4   279. 80,000

280. 300,000   281. 100,000   282. 100   283. 3,000,000

284. 300   285. 5,000,000   286. 40   287. 6,000,000

288. 900.0   289. 1   290. 60,000   291. 7

292. 300   293. 20,000   294. 4   295. 40,000

296. 7,000,000   297. 4,000,000   298. 90,000   299. 20,000

300. 10   301. 800   302. 9   303. 70

304. 80,000   305. 700,000   306. 4   307. 10

308. 200,000   309. 800   310. 900   311. 600,000

Page 42: Multiplication Word Problems

312. 96	313. 140	314. 40	315. 304	316. 112	317. 120
318. 340	319. 21	320. 133	321. 323	322. 28	323. 60
324. 60	325. 160	326. 34	327. 20	328. 208	329. 340
330. 144	331. 162	332. 210	333. 132	334. 72	335. 289
336. 77	337. 136	338. 342	339. 143	340. 234	341. 18

Page 52: Division Word Problems

342. 34	343. 32	344. 78	345. 24	346. 33	347. 90
348. 8	349. 35	350. 325	351. 5	352. 96	353. 57
354. 36	355. 67	356. 26	357. 90	358. 42	359. 35
360. 20	361. 81	362. 60	363. 17	364. 45	365. 82
366. 18	367. 97	368. 38	369. 40	370. 54	371. 19